SHW

ALLEN COUNTY PUBLIC LIBRARY

3 1833 03089 658

D0975116

001.9 W41e
Weeks, David.
Eccentrics : a study
  sanity and strangen

AUG 1 5 1997

ALLEN COUNTY PUBLIC LIBRARY
FORT WAYNE, INDIANA 46802

You-may return this book to any location of
the Allen County Public Library

DEMCO

Eccentrics

A STUDY OF SANITY AND STRANGENESS

DR. DAVID WEEKS AND JAMIE JAMES

Allen County Public Library
900 Webster Street
PO Box 2270
Fort Wayne, IN 46801-2270

Copyright © 1995 by David Weeks and Jamie James

All rights reserved under International and
Pan-American Copyright Conventions. Published in
the United States by Villard Books, a division
of Random House, Inc., New York.

This work was originally published in Great Britain by Weidenfeld & Nicolson,
a division of the Orion Publishing Group, London.

VILLARD BOOKS is a registered trademark of Random House, Inc.

Library of Congress Cataloging-in-Publication Data

Weeks, David Joseph.
Eccentrics: a study of sanity and strangeness /
David Weeks and Jamie James.—1st ed. p. cm.
ISBN 0-394-56565-7
1. Eccentrics and eccentricities—United States—Biography. 2. Eccentrics and
eccentricities—Biography.   I. James, Jamie. II. Title.
CT9990.W348   1995 ˙
001.9—dc20   95-1857

Manufactured in the United States of America
24689753
First U.S. Edition
Book design by Jo Anne Metsch

For our parents

ACKNOWLEDGMENTS

THE AUTHORS WOULD LIKE TO ACKNOWLEDGE THE GENEROUS HELP they have received from the following: Dr. Patch Adams, Dr. Kirsty Anderson, Professor Nancy Andreasen, Isaac Asimov, Josef Astor, Ian Baillie, Geraldine Bedell, Dr. Halla Beloff, Dr. John Beloff, Dr. Brian Bett, Jill Birrell, Dr. William Boyd, Chris Brand, Dr. Donald Broadbent, John Brockman, Mary Bryden, Eric Burke, Lindsley Cameron, Anthony Cheetham, Dr. Jonathan Chick, Professor Anthony Clare, John Clark, Professor Mikaly Csikszentmihalyi, Vincent Egan, Ronald Faux, Sir Nicholas Fairbairn, QC, MP, Gerald Flavin, Dr. David Fontana, David Fratkin, Hugh Freeman, Bridget Freier, Peter Gabriel, Gillian Glover, Zenya Hamada, Anna Hodson, Brenda Houghton, Derek Hudson, Jo Ann Jacobsen, Dr. R. D. Laing, Dr. Donald Low, Ralph McGuire, Victoria McKee, Katinka Matson, Spike Milligan, Marilyn Minden, Professor Robert Morris, Dr. Paul Morrison, Melanne Mueller, Sandy Orr, Dr. Linus Pauling, Dr. André Phanjoo, Dr. Ian Pullen, Harmon L. Remmel, David

Rosenthal, Dr. Hilary Roxborough, Dr. David St Clair, Susan Schiffer, Joan Scobey, Rhea Shedden, Helen Simpson, Dr. B. F. Skinner, Joan Staples-Baum, Kirk Stirling, Corrine Streich, Carol Sturm, Professor Digby Tantam, Teri Noel Towe, Dr. Peter Tyrer, Dr. David Warden, John Graham White, Agnes Wright, Dr. Sula Wolff, and the redoubtable Tom Ward, aviator.

Special thanks for Kate Ward, researcher extraordinaire, who did much of the extensive interviewing and fieldwork.

We reserve final acknowledgment and warmest gratitude for all the eccentrics who participated, with such patience, enthusiasm, and ingenuity, in the study on which this book is based.

CONTENTS

Eccentrics

INTRODUCTION:

A Golden Age of Weirdness

That so few now dare to be eccentric, marks the chief danger of our time.

—*John Stuart Mill,* On Liberty

IT IS USUALLY ASSUMED, ERRONEOUSLY, THAT THE UNITED STATES HAS never been a monarchy. From 1859 to 1880, an English Jew named Joshua Abraham Norton was the emperor of the United States. His accession to the American throne was proclaimed by an edict published in the *San Francisco Bulletin* on September 17, 1859:

> At the peremptory request and desire of a large majority of the citizens of the United States, I, Joshua A. Norton, declare and proclaim myself Emperor of these United States; and in virtue of the authority thereby in me vested, do hereby order and direct the representatives of the different states of the Union to assemble in Musical Hall, of this city, on the

3

first day of February next, then and there to make such alterations in the existing laws of the Union as may ameliorate the evils under which the country is laboring and thereby cause confidence to exist, both at home and abroad, both in our stability and in our integrity.

[Signed]
Norton I, Emperor of the United States and
Protector of Mexico.

Born in London in 1815 and raised in South Africa, Norton made a small fortune during the California Gold Rush speculating in property. In 1853 he gambled a quarter of a million dollars on an effort to corner the rice market in San Francisco, buying and stockpiling all the available supply, and thereby artificially inflating the price. However, just as he was about to cash in, several ships laden with rice sailed into the bay, glutting the market. Prices plummeted, and Norton went bust. He was soon reduced to working in a sweatshop and living in a seedy rooming house.

Most people would have been daunted by such a reversal of fortune, but not the doughty Norton. He discovered his true vocation: ruling an empire. He began confiding to his friends that he was really Norton I, emperor of California. In 1856, the same year he filed for bankruptcy, he also issued his first imperial edict, imposing a monthly tax of fifty cents on sympathetic merchants in San Francisco to bankroll the fledgling empire. By 1859 he had decided that California was not big enough for him, and he annexed the whole United States.

He became instantly famous. He suspended the Constitution and dissolved both the Republican and the Democratic political parties on the grounds that "their existence engendered dissensions." He printed his own money in twenty-five- and fifty-cent denominations, which was accepted freely in most shops and restaurants in San Francisco. Yet as emperor he felt that he was entitled to more, and he tried to negotiate loans of several million dollars from the banks, which found tactful ways of evading the imperial demands.

Norton took his responsibilities seriously. For more than twenty years he patrolled the streets, seeing to it that the sidewalks were unobstructed and the streetcars ran on time. He never missed a session of the state Senate, where a chair was reserved for him, and he attended a different church every week so as to avoid sectarian strife in the empire. The emperor was a benevolent despot for the most part, but when his authority was challenged he responded with an iron fist: when Maximilian assumed the throne of Mexico, which was an imperial protectorate, Norton sentenced him to death as a usurper.

The emperor always wore a blue military uniform with golden epaulettes, which had been given to him by army officers, with a tall, plumed beaver hat, a sword, and a rosette. In 1869, when his uniform became shabby, he issued another edict:

> Know ye whom it may concern that We, Norton I, Emperor
> *Dei gratia* of the United States and Protector of Mexico,
> have heard serious complaints from our adherents and all
> that our imperial wardrobe is a national disgrace, and even
> His Majesty the King of Pain has had his sympathy excited

so far as to offer us a suit of clothing, which we have a delicacy in accepting. Therefore we warn those whose duty it is to attend to these affairs that their scalps are in danger if our said need is unheeded.

The city's Board of Supervisors, mindful of its scalps, appropriated the money to buy him a new uniform. The emperor, touched by this gesture of fealty, knighted the whole board.

The King of Pain referred to in the emperor's edict was a fellow street royal, a patent-medicine salesman who wore scarlet underwear, a heavy velour robe, and a stovepipe hat decorated with ostrich feathers. The king rode a black coach drawn by six white horses—considerably more horsepower than the crowded city streets required.

San Francisco, always renowned as a capital of the freakish and fantastical, had its golden age of weirdness in those post–Gold Rush years. Another of Emperor Norton's subjects was Oofty Goofty, the Wild Man of Borneo, who walked about swathed in furs, making strange animal cries. He supported himself by allowing passersby to kick him for ten cents, to cane him for twenty-five cents, and to hit him with a baseball bat for fifty cents. The boxing champion John L. Sullivan, getting his half-dollar's worth, sent Oofty Goofty to the hospital with a fractured spine.

There was also a phrenologist named Uncle Freddie Coombs, who bore a striking resemblance to George Washington. He took to wearing knee breeches, a powdered wig, and a tricorn hat, and went about the city with a banner proclaiming himself to be "Washington the Second." Montgomery Street was the beat of the Great Unknown, an impeccably attired, vaguely theatrical gentleman with a gold-headed cane, who took a stroll every afternoon, mysteriously averting his gaze and speaking to no one. After many years of this enigma, there was a public reception in Pacific Hall, where it was revealed to everyone who was interested enough to pay twenty-five cents that the Great Unknown was a retired German tailor named William Frohm.

In their lifetimes Emperor Norton, the King of Pain, Oofty Goofty, Uncle Freddie Coombs, and the Great Unknown were regarded as harmless eccentrics, a source of delight and even a sort of strange asset to the community. Today they would be declared to be suffering from any number of well-defined mental illnesses, vigorously battered with tests and physical treatments, diagnosed, tranquilized, stabilized, and forced to be "normal," whether they wanted it or not.

Yet there is no evidence that these men were unhappy, or that their lives would have been improved in any way by being compelled to surrender their eccentricities and conform. If Emperor Norton had been "cured," he might have had a normal, conventional, dull career as a clerk or salesman—a miserable comedown for a man who had wielded the scepter. His life would have been impoverished, and so would that of the society he lived in. When Norton died in 1880, the *San Francisco Chronicle* ran the headline "Le Roi Est Mort." The police were summoned to ensure order in the huge crowds of people who came to the funeral parlor to pay their last respects to their beloved monarch. All flags in the city were flown at half-mast. Thirty thousand mourners attended the lavish graveside service, and many more than that turned out to see the funeral procession pass through the streets of San Francisco to the Masonic Cemetery.

Emperor Norton and his court pose a challenge to the assumption that underlies all modern psychology, that we know more than we used to about the mind, and therefore that we are doing things better now. In fact a strong case could be made that even though nineteenth-century Californians knew nothing about brain-cell synapses or neurotransmitters, delusional grandiose mania or borderline syndromes, in humanitarian terms they got it much more right than we do now.

Why is that? Precisely what does it mean, in the first place, to say that Emperor Norton and the others were eccentric? The dictionary tells us that an eccentric is someone who deviates from the conventional or established norm, who is different from the rest of us—hardly a definition that is likely to satisfy a trained psychologist. That description applies just as well to a criminal or a person with a birth defect.

What does science have to say on the subject? Ten years ago, when I first began asking these questions, I undertook a thorough search for some answers through the vast, forbidding tundra known as the scientific literature. One would expect that abnormal or clinical psychology, which has produced definitive treatises on every conceivable deviation from normal behavior, must surely have established a sound, widely tested profile of the eccentric, one that carefully distinguishes the syndrome from other, harmful forms of mental aberration. Yet in fact there is next to nothing to be found on the subject of eccentricity in modern scholarly literature. Because eccentrics tend to be healthier than most people, they rarely seek the services of the medical profession, and the medical profession, as a rule, is not very interested in those who do not seek it out.

In the field of experimental psychology, it is an open secret that we have learned a great deal about how penniless undergraduates perform in narrow and sometimes deliberately deceptive experiments, while psychiatrists, on the other hand, know about every possible variation in the behavior of people who have had mental breakdowns. The rub, from the scientific point of view, is that those two groups rarely overlap, so most of the theoretical knowledge obtained by the experimental psychologists is useless to the psychiatrists who are dealing with patients. Meanwhile, almost *nobody* is studying adult nonpatients, the vast bulk of humanity.

Of the four best-known textbooks on psychiatry, three make no mention of eccentricity. The fourth describes it, cryptically, as a form of "predominantly inadequate or passive psychopathy," adding that it is "usually difficult to distinguish the symptoms of eccentricity from schizophrenic manifestations." These summary statements are tossed off with nonchalance, and there is no mention of the fact that they are based upon a database of zero patients and research subjects, and upon clinical observations that are at best haphazard.

Thus it appeared to me that actual scientific knowledge about eccentrics was virtually nonexistent. Nature abhors a vacuum, and so does a scientist: since no study of eccentricity existed, I decided to begin my own. It occurred to me that it would be a great advantage to psychology to have a basic understanding of the thought processes of people who come to regard themselves, and who are regarded by others, as eccentric, if only to help distinguish their behavior from certain forms of mental illness. Such a study would also be an ideal way to learn about illogical thought processes, and it might help us to understand more about the deep human mystery of schizophrenia. Furthermore, given the frequent association of eccentricity with genius, the ability to conceive startlingly original artistic and scientific breakthroughs, it seemed to be an obviously worthwhile subject for psychological research. For the annals of eccentricity include, in addition to Emperor Norton and Oofty Goofty, such names as William Blake, Alexander Graham Bell, Emily Dickinson, Charlie Chaplin, and Ludwig Wittgenstein, not to mention Albert Einstein and Howard Hughes. If we could gain even the barest glimpse into how all those people came to be the way they were, it might just help the rest of us to be more creative, more original: better at being ourselves.

The study began in 1984 in Edinburgh, where I am a principal clinical psychologist at the Royal Edinburgh Hospital, and it soon attracted media attention throughout Great Britain, which greatly enlarged the sample. As more eccentrics learned about what my research team and I were doing, they began to come to us. Before long we initiated a study of eccentrics in the United States, as well. The sample ultimately included more than a thousand eccentrics, most of them Americans, who were interviewed by me and my research associates over the course of ten years. Our findings are the basis of this book.

The qualities that characterize the eccentric, and their antitheses, are best thought of not simply as positive (and negative) values but rather as continuums. For instance, as we begin to sketch the outlines of what constitutes eccentricity, we might advance the obvious premise that it is not normal. Human behavior ranges from absolute conformity, at the normal end of the spectrum, to utterly bizarre nonconformity at the opposite end. Thus, for example, a man who wears pink socks every day of the year, regardless of whether he is wearing a business suit or Bermuda shorts, demonstrates behavior toward the eccentric end of the continuum. Yet if he exhibits no other eccentric traits, then we might decide that he ought not to be classified as a true eccentric.

Exactly how much deviation from the norm it takes to qualify as a true eccentric is a vexed issue: until we have established qualitatively what eccentricity is, then it is impossible to contemplate the matter quantitatively. For eccentricity is a trait that everyone partakes of to a lesser or greater extent: absolute, uniform conformity, if it existed, would itself be a kind of eccentricity. Therefore, we cannot take for granted the concept of an objectively verifiable control, a behavioral norm by which to define aberration. The question of what constitutes normality is among the most subjective issues in life. We have all had the experience of talking with a friend who tells us that he has just met someone with the most bizarre habit—only to hear described something that we ourselves do or might wish to do.

Social factors, too, are potent. Even in the global village, what is normal in New York or London will seem very strange to the Tahitian or the Nigerian, and vice versa. Nor is it necessary to cast the net so wide. What is acceptable behavior for someone in Los Angeles might seem passing strange to a person living in Glasgow, although the two of them may see eye to eye on the question of what constitutes eccentricity and what does not. Just because the surfer does not himself wear a kilt, that does not mean that he will find it eccentric in a Scotsman—or a socialite from Orange County, California—to do so.

Moreover, there is a wide variation in the spectrum of deviations that societies will tolerate. In Japan a greater degree of conformity is expected than in the United States or Great Britain, while in a preindustrial society such as that of the Aleut or the Indians of the South American rain forest, virtually every aspect of human behavior follows a rigid pattern. The same differential also exists within our society: the reason places like New York and San Francisco have become known as havens for nonconformists is because they are more tolerant of such behavior than are the small towns of America. In Britain, on the other hand, that sort of stratification tends to be more a question of class: Dame Edith Sitwell was able to indulge in bizarre behavior—and write a highly eccentric book called *English Eccentrics*—because her social position permitted it, whereas the same activities would have been self-destructive on the part of a rural clergyman's daughter.

ECCENTRICS

Since my research is, scientifically speaking, the first word on the subject, it is a certainty that it will not be the last. When you undertake the first scientific study of any subject, you find a Catch-22 looming: since you are working in the dark, without fundamental principles to guide you, any preconceptions you might have are suspect and ought to be regarded, at least initially, with stringent skepticism. Any criteria you may establish will be arbitrary, and therefore unscientific. It is no good to say that everyone knows what eccentricity is, if we can't define it: that may be true, but it is not a sound way to establish a clinical definition. One man's eccentricity is another man's acceptable variation.

And what if the person doing the defining is eccentric himself, as was the case with Dame Edith Sitwell? Even in the notoriously squishy land of theoretical psychology, science demands a certain standard of objectivity. When someone makes a study of schizophrenia or memory loss, there are preexisting studies with objective correlatives that have established criteria and standards as the basis for the discussion. A new study may overturn all the accepted wisdom on the subject, but even a limited amount of scholarly give and take provides some measure of objectivity. In the case of my study of eccentrics, however, we were cutting it out of whole cloth. The study was thus necessarily more in the nature of mass observation than a scientific survey in the strict sense: it was descriptive rather than analytical.

At the beginning of the study we found that the question "What is eccentricity?" was best answered by considering some of the things it is not. It is a common article of received wisdom that there is a fine line between genius and madness. One of the most common misconceptions about eccentricity is that it is a mild form of madness—in other words, that eccentric behavior is a symptom of mental illness. Yet that formula brings us straight back to Emperor Norton and his companions in strangeness: illness implies suffering and the need of a cure, yet even a casual observation of most eccentrics undermines such a conclusion.

Especially great care must be taken to distinguish between eccentricity and neurosis, lest we commit the error the authors of that psychiatric textbook warned us against. While it is true that the behavior of neurotics is also aberrant, there is an enormous qualitative difference between the two. Neurotics are repetitively dysphoric: they suffer from panic attacks, phobias, and high anxiety levels on account of their differentness, and therefore they want to be cured. Neurosis is often thrust upon the sufferer from the outside; it is an unwanted difficulty in life.

Eccentricity, on the other hand, is taken on at least partly by free choice, and is something positive and pleasurable to the individual. Simply put, neurotics are miserable because they think they're not as good as everyone else, while eccentrics know they're different and glory in it. An eccentric knows he is right and, far from wanting to change his ways, is likely to wish to convert everyone else to his way of thinking. A philosopher might say that Joshua Norton was not wrong in his conviction that he was the emperor of the United States; he simply failed to convince the American people that they were his subjects.

An even more essential distinction needs to be drawn

between eccentricity and psychosis, though it may sometimes seem a blurry one to the lay observer. One common trait of eccentrics is that they often experience mental images that are more vivid than those of normal people. Some extreme eccentrics have visions, which is a not uncommon symptom of schizophrenia. The important distinction is that the schizophrenic has no control over his visions and the voices he hears: they intrude themselves upon him forcibly and give rise to a terrifying sensation of powerlessness. The eccentric, on the other hand, is likely to find his visions a source of delight, and he has much more control over them. The psychotic state severely disrupts thought processes, leaving the person dysfunctional, whereas the eccentric's brain usually functions perfectly well—it just does so in peculiar and largely unknown (but not unknowable) ways.

Eccentricity can also mimic certain personality disorders, as illustrated by two examples. First, in cases of hysterical personality disorder the patient sometimes behaves flamboyantly, drawing attention to himself in public in extravagant, histrionic ways. Second, a person with a schizoid personality prefers to be on his own, showing an extreme aversion to groups, a tendency that usually results in a remarkable concentration on strange, obsessive hobbies. The traits of both these disorders may be detected in the behavior of some eccentrics. While many eccentrics are known for their flamboyant public personalities (Emperor Norton being one excellent example) and others have obsessive hobbies, the same fundamental distinction must be made: the person suffering from the personality disorder is dysfunctional and ordinarily has little choice in the matter, while for the eccentric it is a positive, pleasurable experience. A schizoid person and an eccentric might both become obsessive butterfly collectors, say, but whereas the schizoid will do anything to satisfy the compulsion to collect, and may feel threatened on all sides by impediments to his collecting, for the eccentric it will be a source of delight, an avocation to which he freely devotes time and energy. The one is reactive, bringing stress to himself and to others; the other is creative and joyful.

We should emphasize at the outset that even though eccentricity is not a form of mental illness, eccentrics have no special immunity from diseases of the mind. Just as you would expect in any large group of people, regardless of how it was chosen, some of the subjects in the study suffered from mental illnesses. Yet we found by administering standard diagnostic tests that eccentrics actually have a higher general level of mental health than the population at large. Original thinking, it seems, may be better for you than dull conformity.

We love eccentrics, and yet we are profoundly ambivalent about them. Our collective imagination is piqued by the bizarre behavior of someone like Howard Hughes, the richest man in the world (or close enough), who lived the last days of his life like a mystical hermit. We are fascinated by them, yet we may also be simultaneously repelled and threatened. Eccentrics have thrown off the constraints of normal life to let themselves do exactly as they please—and anyone who doesn't like it be damned. The rest of us are vaguely unsettled by that degree of freedom. Why should we continue to groom ourselves properly and comport ourselves according to social convention, while those who flout convention seem to be having the time of their life, and also, in many cases, enjoying perfect health and great personal and professional success?

That ambiguity reflects society's ambivalence toward anyone who is different. Most of us have made peace with people who are of a different race or religion, with homosexuals, with the very short or very fat, but it is an uneasy peace, whether or not we admit it. There is something deep inside that yearns to be reassured that we are "right," and those who are fundamentally different threaten that inner conservative streak. Eccentrics are especially troubling to us because they cannot be easily pigeonholed, and often pass unnoticed among the rest of us, for while some eccentrics proclaim their differences by bizarre dress and grooming, most do not.

Yet it is precisely that serendipitous aspect of eccentricity that delights us. We love the idea of encountering the outlandish and whimsical in our lives, even though we may fear to find it in ourselves. One of the most dramatic proofs of our ambivalence toward eccentrics occurred three years after I began my study. A talk show in Newcastle invited me to bring along some of the subjects of my study for a program. I brought with me Screaming Lord Sutch, an aristocratic rock star manqué, and perennial parliamentary candidate of the Monster Raving Loony party, of which he is the founder and leader; John Slater, who has walked barefoot from Land's End to John O'Groats in his pajamas, and appointed his dog, Tiny, a 250-pound sheepdog, to be the executive director of his tour-guide company; Stanley Unwin, an eighty-one-year-old man whose obsession is to speak gobbledygook that makes sense, combining malapropisms, puns, and words of his own coinage in an absurdist, rococo stream of consciousness that only a crack grammarian could hope to disentangle; a native Londoner who now calls himself Chief Shiloh and habitually wears the full regalia of the Cherokee nation; and Ann Atkin, an elfin-looking woman whose house in Devon is populated by 7,500 garden gnomes. She brought to the studio gnome hats she had knitted and offered them to the other guests on the show.

The first half of the show, before we came on, was devoted to school discipline, a subject that was solemnly discussed by three gray-suited headmasters, the most staid group of right-thinking establishment guardians you could ever have assembled. When they met the eccentrics in the greenroom, they were fascinated yet repelled, and perhaps even a bit frightened. When Ann Atkin offered them gnome hats, they avoided her as though she had a contagious disease. Yet they could not keep their eyes off these strange, individualistic people, who were obviously enjoying themselves and one another enormously. I remember thinking at the time what a pity it was that those old duffers couldn't loosen up and enjoy such an interesting and utterly harmless group of people. I suspect that they wanted to, but the fear of the unknown kept them firmly on their own side of the room.

This book is an attempt to bridge that gap. Psychology now takes itself, its image, and its methods far too seriously.

It has largely turned its back on the excitement of guess-work, on the wonderment of speculation, which is fundamental to doing any real science. Human evolution needs human eccentricity. Although, in an age of increasing standardization and homogeneity, psychologists may react suspiciously to peculiar ideas and idiosyncratic people, they should keep their minds open to the rebellious fun of those who deviate from the norm.

In *Walden,* Thoreau wrote, "If a man does not keep pace with his companions, perhaps it is because he hears a different drummer. Let him step to the music which he hears." Let us follow Thoreau's advice, and see where it may lead us.

ONE

The study

Subjectivity is the characteristic of perspectives and biographies, the characteristic of giving the view of the world from a certain place. . . . The particulars forming one perspective are connected together primarily by simultaneity; those forming one biography, primarily by the existence of direct time-relations between them. To these are to be added relations derivable from the laws of perspective. In all this we are clearly not in the region of psychology, as commonly understood; yet we are also hardly in the region of physics.

—*Bertrand Russell,*
The Analysis of Mind

HAVING DECIDED TO UNDERTAKE A SYSTEMATIC STUDY OF ECCEN-tricity, the first challenge was to find the eccentrics. They tend to take themselves seriously, and there was a danger that they would not want to be part of a study in which they might fear they would be associated with mental illness or ridiculed. The economic motive—offering prospective sub-jects money to participate—might not prove to be effective, for we found that eccentrics tend to be idealistic and are rarely motivated by greed. Moreover, normal surveying methods were not applicable, because eccentrics are rare and geographically spread very wide.

Since we couldn't rely upon the ordinary methods for recruiting research subjects, I decided to advertise. I was confident that I could turn up a large sample that way, but it presented the problem of self-selection: the volunteer would be deciding for himself, at least initially, if he was eccentric. Yet there did seem to be a logical failsafe built into the method, for would there not be something eccen-tric about any person who answered an advertisement sol-iciting eccentrics? What evolved out of necessity, if not actual desperation, was a new survey method, which I called multimedia survey sampling.

We began by placing a number of discreet advertise-ments on index cards in a range of establishments in the Edinburgh area: pubs, wine bars, launderettes, libraries, su-permarkets, universities, and so forth. Every effort was made to ensure that the locations of these advertisements were as representative as possible, so that they would be seen by as broad a cross section of the population as possi-ble. They read, simply, "Eccentric? If you feel that you might be, contact Dr. David Weeks at the Royal Edinburgh Hospi-tal," and gave my telephone number.

Soon after this phase began, a journalist spotted one of the cards that we had posted in the University Staff Club; I was particularly interested in the absent-minded-professor type of eccentric. That led to an article in a local newspaper, which in turn led to a longer article in *The Scotsman,* Scotland's most prestigious daily newspaper. Both articles included the text of the advertisement with my telephone number.

Most scientists, whether they admit it or not, love publicity. But in this case, in addition to the normal, almost childish fascination I felt at seeing my name and face in the newspaper, there was a serious purpose. Every time another story about the study was published, we would get a flurry of calls from eccentrics who were intrigued by what we were doing. Once we realized how effective the method was, we decided to try to control our mass-media sampling, to make it as comprehensive as the index-card campaign had been. In order to get wider coverage, and thereby to attract a representative sample of subjects, we needed to break through to the mass-circulation press. We sent out press releases to every national newspaper in Great Britain, but before long many reporters were finding the story for themselves. As we expected, a certain amount of brainless satire accompanied the coverage in the tabloids, but we didn't mind that so long as they spelled my name right and included the telephone number, which they usually did.

Radio and television interviews followed, which further ensured the representativeness of the sample. We received excellent coverage, with programs on all four BBC radio channels as well as a number of local stations. Stories about the research appeared amid pop music, at the end of the national news, on talk shows, on medical programs. Various times of day were covered, from early-morning breakfast television and radio to late-night call-in shows.

The American press picked up the story, which helped to transform the study into a transatlantic phenomenon. Syndicated features in *The New York Times, The Wall Street Journal, Los Angeles Times, San Francisco Chronicle,* and *International Herald Tribune* spread the word about our study throughout the English-speaking world. The contents of our mailbag at the hospital became increasingly bizarre and exotic.

An exploratory investigation in any field can exclude no potential subject at the outset, on any grounds whatsoever. We realized that, since we had no criteria to serve as the basis for the study, we had to maintain as receptive and open-minded an attitude as possible. No stone could be left unturned, no lead not followed up, for the more representative the subject pool, the more reliable and valid the study's findings would be. The grand total of readers, listeners, and viewers reached by the basic appeal, based on combined circulation and audience-research figures, came to 110 million people in the United States and 30 million in Great Britain. Short of the national census, we believe it was the largest population group ever sampled by a team of psychologists.

These numbers include every person who read or heard about my research, which might seem to be a somewhat superficial contact. Yet even so glancing a connection proved to be all that was required to establish communication with hundreds of good potential subjects, and drew in a surprisingly small number of cranks. Most of the telephone calls and letters we received began along these lines: "I saw the article about your research in this morning's paper, and I thought perhaps you might be interested in my extensive research into the syntax of the cat language," or whatever their particular hobbyhorse happened to be. We soon learned that, while eccentrics rarely seek to draw attention to themselves, most of them are eager to share their ideas with others.

Then began the laborious process of winnowing out the true eccentrics who would form the basis of the study. A few respondents eliminated themselves immediately as hoaxers and practical jokers. About 10 percent of the respondents proved to be such mild cases as to be virtually indistinguishable from noneccentrics. Some respondents were just lonely people who wanted someone to talk to.

After we had acquired some experience with eccentrics, we began to realize that a self-selecting sample had an inherent limitation. While most eccentrics are outgoing and willing to talk about themselves, some are not. It emerged that, proportionately, there are about as many shy eccentrics as shy noneccentrics, people with a completely normal timidity about coming forward. In some cases they resented the eccentric label; in others they feared that associating themselves with the study might hurt them professionally. To bring these people into the fold, even if anonymously, we relied upon the oldest form of networking known to humankind: word of mouth. Social scientists sometimes refer to this technique as snowballing. It is especially apt for recruiting people who are, by society's standards, outsiders.

ECCENTRICS

We received several responses from friends and family members like "My uncle is too shy to call you himself, but he is a true eccentric." We found that with a careful, reassuring approach to bashful eccentrics we could usually entice them into the study. In addition, eccentrics are sometimes friendly with other eccentrics, and several subjects were brought in that way. Such third-party recommendations gave a certain added cachet to the identification of the individual as an eccentric.

After we had eliminated all the obvious mistakes and instances of deception from the initial sample, we had 789 potential eccentrics, 309 men and 480 women. Eventually the number grew to more than a thousand. The subjects ranged across the entire social spectrum, including a deputy chairman of a large industrial firm, a senior judge, a puppeteer, a chiropractor, and an unemployed poet. There were several self-made millionaires and a few cave-dwelling hermits. There were housewives and sorceresses, university professors and factory workers, computer scientists and established artists and writers. They ranged in age from sixteen to ninety-two, with an average age of forty-five years. The subjects tended to be predominantly middle-class and somewhat better educated than the general population, with a mean of fourteen years of education.

By applying standard statistical analysis to the numbers we came up with in the study, we concluded that the prevalence of classic, full-time eccentrics in the population could be estimated at 1 in 10,000. Owing to the unorthodox sampling techniques and the softness of our initial definition, the margin of error might be as much as plus or minus 50 percent. In other words, the true eccentric condition could be as rare as 1 in 15,000, or relatively more common at 1 in 5,000. However, we were surprised to find that there were more eccentrics in the Minneapolis–St. Paul region, per capita, than in any other area of the United States.

Now the real work began. We talked with each of the subjects in one-on-one interviews that lasted at least ninety minutes, though many of them went on far longer: eccentrics tend to be chatty people. Whenever possible, we conducted the interviews informally, in the subjects' homes, so they would be more relaxed, more confident, and therefore under less stress, thus making their responses as spontaneous as possible under the circumstances.

We began by asking questions intended to discover if there were any obvious symptoms of mental disorder, to create a quick sketch of the personality of the subject, and to gather background information. Some of the questions were very specific, to test hypotheses we were entertaining at the moment, but most of them were quite general, because of the exploratory nature of the study. The questions were open-ended; that is, there were no "correct" responses, nor could they be answered by "yes" or "no." The intention was rather to draw out long, descriptive answers, which would reveal as much as possible about the subjects. We explicitly set out to grasp not only the opinions and beliefs of our subjects but also their *ways* of thinking and believing. Many of them felt compelled to explain themselves, to make sense of their unusual way of life. As one subject put it, "I have to speak for myself." We ambitiously set out to elicit the full repertoire of concepts, valid or not, held by all of them.

In order to gather as much data as possible, we also gave the subjects standard personality evaluations, IQ tests, and examinations used by psychiatrists to diagnose schizophrenia and other mental illnesses. We weren't quite sure initially what we would actually do with all that information, but as the database grew, it created a full descriptive psychological portrait of the subjects. We tape-recorded all the interviews so that we could analyze the subjects' speech patterns, and that, too, gave us some important insights.

The study became a group portrait of people as varied as society at large, yet with many common traits. A profile emerged with fifteen characteristics that applied to most eccentrics, ranging from the obvious to the trivial. We found that an eccentric may be described in the following ways, more or less in descending order of frequency:

- nonconforming;
- creative;
- strongly motivated by curiosity;
- idealistic: he wants to make the world a better place and the people in it happier;
- happily obsessed with one or more hobbyhorses (usually five or six);
- aware from early childhood that he is different;
- intelligent;
- opinionated and outspoken, convinced that he is right and that the rest of the world is out of step;

- noncompetitive, not in need of reassurance or reinforcement from society;
- unusual in his eating habits and living arrangements;
- not particularly interested in the opinions or company of other people, except in order to persuade them to his— the correct—point of view;
- possessed of a mischievous sense of humor;
- single;
- usually the eldest or an only child; and
- a bad speller.

The first five characteristics listed here are the most important and apply to virtually every eccentric. Nonconformity is, of course, the principal defining trait of the breed, and any of the subjects we studied could be used to illustrate it, but perhaps none of them is quite as clear-cut a case of nonconformity as Marvin Staples, an ebullient Chippewa Indian from Minnesota, who walks everywhere backward. He said that the idea came to him after a three-day fast. He was inspired by a scene from the film *Little Big Man,* in which an Indian warrior is embarrassed because his life has been saved by a white man, and he lives backward until he regains his honor in battle. Staples said that living life in reverse made him feel younger and cured him of chronic backache and arthritis in his knees. "The Hyokas Indians used to walk backward," he said, "trusting the Great Spirit to catch them if they fell. The Hyokas and the Sioux also did things backward to make people laugh and to forget about their problems."

The backward life has deepened him spiritually as well,

he said. "I used to want more and more, but now I think about how I can get by with less. I don't worry about the future. Once I thought about running for president. Presidents do a lot of things backward." Staples broke the previous record for walking backward, which according to the *Guinness Book of World Records* (a mother lode of eccentrics) was held by Plennie Wingo, of Abilene, Texas. Wingo began walking backward on April 15, 1931, in Santa Monica, California, and reached Istanbul on October 24, 1932.

Another eccentric in our study, Darla Shaw, from western Connecticut, exhibits what might be called global eccentricity: she leads nearly every aspect of her life in a nonconforming way. She believes that it's immoral to throw anything away, so she still owns everything she has ever purchased or been given. In addition to vast amounts of what most people would consider to be ordinary garbage, she owns a good stock of theatrical costumes, a life-sized Santa on skis, a papier-mâché mermaid, a brace of stuffed alligators, and a portable shower that doubles as a telephone booth. Darla's hoard of earthly possessions finally grew to such vast proportions that she bought an abandoned opera house in order to have room for everything.

Wherever she goes, Darla pushes around a grocery cart with headlights that is loaded with a miscellany of objects from her collection. Among many other hobbies, she plays in a kazoo band. In winter she wears a fireman's coat. Darla is a great entertainer, but she can't cook very well so she gives what she calls "canned-food parties." She serves canned stew with canned beans, followed by canned fruit and canned pudding. One summer she had a Wimbledon party: beneath a striped yellow-and-white canopy, she served 7-Up and ice cream with strawberries (canned, of course), and dressed as a member of the British royal family. She gave the papier-mâché mermaid a full Viking funeral on a lake near her home. She and her family eulogized the mermaid, put it aboard a small dinghy, and set it afire. The mourners sang "The Volga Boatman" as the blazing mermaid drifted across the lake.

At the root of Marvin Staples's and Darla's nonconformity is a persistent refusal to accept anything as given. They question assumptions that the rest of us take for granted. Darla expressed this state of mind concisely in her statement to us: "Each of us is born a unique individual. You don't need to follow the crowd. The sky is the limit, so don't let anyone clip your wings. I tend to perceive events in a slightly askew fashion quite naturally. By taking risks, some new excitement or enlightenment may be brought into life at any time." While the results of that sort of extreme nonconformity may seem absurd to others, for the eccentric there is a sense of freedom from the constraints of everyday life. The rest of the world believes that there is only one direction to walk, that firemen's coats are for firemen and a lady should wear a tweed coat in the winter; but for eccentrics those are just boring rules that exist only to be flouted.

Creativity is at the heart of eccentricity. One of the principal reasons eccentrics continually challenge the established order is because they want to experiment, to try out new ways of doing things. That quality is most conspicuous in artists and scientists, who are significantly more likely to be eccentric than the rest of us. The study included seventy-five artists, whose lives are, obviously, devoted to creative activity, as well as many inventors, who use their brain-power to bring into existence entirely new and presumably useful machines. But some of our eccentrics were driven, it seems, not by traditional aesthetic or scientific impulses but rather by a powerful need to create in its purest, generalized form. One such person is John Ward of Northamptonshire, who describes himself as a junkist. He constructs fantastical machines from other people's rubbish. On the day the Prince and Princess of Wales got married, he celebrated by welding together three bathtubs to make a catamaran for his four children.

For months afterward, Ward tinkered away with piles of household junk on his new masterpiece. Well-meaning neighbors and total strangers who had heard about him turned up on his doorstep with broken household appliances. Local businesses contributed hundreds of broken machines. Finally, Ward unveiled the fruits of his hard work: a functioning (if the word may be applied to something that has no conceivable use) contraption he called a moon buggy, constructed from an old bed, a number of hair dryers and vacuum cleaners, a wicker linen basket, a tumble dryer, a baby carriage, and hundreds of odds and ends cannibalized from other objects, with sirens and flashing lights. "It's a shining example of a load of old rubbish," he told us. "There's so much waste in the world, I like to put rubbish to good use. A lot of people say I'm into my second childhood, but I don't think I ever got out of my first. Getting carried away is the bother of invention."

Al Joyner of Virginia Beach, Virginia, rides around town on a contraption that is half bicycle, half rocking horse. "I already had a bike," he told us, "and one day I lay down on the sofa and said to myself, 'I want a horse.' So I bought a rocking horse for fifteen dollars and cut it in half and put it on the bike." He added reflectors to the horse's head, flanks, and hind hooves, lariats to the handlebars, and a strand of pearls around the horse's neck. On one side of the bicycle wheels are hubcaps, adorned with more reflectors, and on the other side a bright orange cymbal with stick-on letters that spell out "DISCO KID." Joyner pulls behind him a milk crate mounted on a golf cart.

Disco, as he calls his horse, is not only an obvious expression of its owner's nonconformity but also a completely original creative work, neither art nor science and of use only to its creator—but a source of great joy to the children of the neighborhood. Yet Disco possesses a numinous, attractive quality; Joyner told us that he is besieged by people who want him to build similar horse-bicycles for them. He receives so many requests to have his photograph taken with Disco that he occasionally has to go into hiding.

Closely allied to creativity is the eccentric's intense curiosity. Most eccentrics told us that they first became aware that they were different from everyone else when they were children, because they were constantly searching for underlying answers. When they asked their parents "Why?" they were never content with "Just because," and even less happy with "Because I said so." Curiosity is the only human motivation that is primarily intellectual; some psychologists call it the intrinsic motivation, because the process of discovery is its own reward. All of us are curious about some things, perhaps intensely curious, but if it becomes too difficult to find the answer, our interest will gradually fade. For the eccentric, however, finding out the answer becomes an obsession. The nineteenth-century British naturalist Charles Waterton, while conducting research in the South American rain forest, spent several months sleeping with a foot dangling out of his hammock, in the hope of experiencing the bite of a vampire bat. He was, he said, "frightfully disappointed" to be left untouched by "the provoking brutes." Waterton has also been plausiby described as the first man to wear a crew cut.

Eccentric inventors exemplify this need to know in its pure form. Many of them have come up with quite useful devices, while others have devoted their lives to inventing absurd, fantastical devices. We interviewed several eccentrics who were bent upon unraveling the mystery of perpetual motion, the inventor's equivalent of the philosopher's stone. Since before the Industrial Revolution, the notion of the perpetual-motion machine (or fuelless engine, as it is now sometimes called) has captured the imagination of thousands of inventors and entrepreneurs, despite the incontrovertible evidence of science that it is impossible. The very notion violates Carnot's First Law of Thermodynamics, the concept of the conservation of energy, and Clausius's Second Law of Thermodynamics, which states that part of the energy of a continuous process is always lost as heat. In any case, nothing in this world is perpetual: rust, friction, and general wear-and-tear put a limit on the life of any mechanical device.

Yet "impossible" is not a word in the eccentric lexicon. Yvonne X (that is her name) builds perpetual-motion machines in her workshop in Westfield, New Jersey. When I visited her, she told me that she had always been an inventor: "When I was a kid, I got so interested in the space race that I started making my own rockets. There was no method to my experiments—I just got a kick out of the explosions. I loved to see my rockets go up. Then my concern about the environment led me to try and invent energy traps like this one."

She led me out to the workshop and proudly pointed at her machine, which looked like something out of a low-budget 1950s science-fiction film. Gleaming stainless-steel cylinders were mounted on a frame along the brick wall. Tubes sprouted from the tops and bottoms, joined together by candelabra-shaped connectors. In the far corner more tubes dripped from the ceiling like plastic spaghetti. In the center was a highly polished silver disk, about the size of a football, mounted on a tripod and suspended by wires. When she switched the machine on, the tubes began twitching as a frothy liquid coursed through them.

While the machine was warming up, she explained its "scientific" basis to me: "This system produces energy without combustion and preserves it safely. The flux of these liquids can be made to create kinetic energy, which can then be changed into cheap electricity. When the disk ascends, we will have power to spare!"

She squeezed a trigger mounted on the machine to activate it. The pipes made a fizzing sound, the liquids changed color, and the tubes began vibrating violently. A deep rumble issued sickeningly from the cylinders, and a gasket blew off like a bullet, splattering test tubes. Then the silver disk, spinning with a gentle hum, began to ascend, faster and faster, until it finally crashed right through the workshop ceiling. I could see the moon shining through the hole it left behind. There was a moment of calm. Yvonne X and I gaped at each other.

Then, as Milton said, all hell broke loose. Behind us a beaker exploded, then another. Sparks came showering out of melting wires. The room was filled with the acrid smells of raw electricity and singed eyebrows (mine). The sprinkler system came on and sprayed the room with warm water. Yvonne turned and hightailed it out of the room, with me treading on her heels and feeling very much like a character in a particularly violent Warner Brothers cartoon. The fire department was soon on the scene. As firemen hosed down the scene of the disaster, Yvonne X was already brainstorming. She told me she was certain she knew what was wrong with the design, and vowed to start over.

That indomitable spirit of hopefulness is almost universal among eccentrics. Not only is their positive outlook expressed in their attitude toward their own life and work but it also frequently extends to a more general spirit of idealism and love of humanity. Such idealism infuses the work of Dr. Patch Adams, a clown doctor who in 1971 founded the Gesundheit Institute in Pocahontas County, West Virginia. Adams, who has a medical degree from the Medical College of Virginia, believes that humor is an integral part of healing, and he frequently dresses as a clown when he practices medicine. He also believes that money has ruined medicine, and he accepts no payment of any kind for treating his patients. He explained his philosophy: "If everyone's life was bathed in friendship, humor, love, creativity, hope, curiosity, and wonder—*wheeee!*—we would need a lot less medicine. It would eliminate Prozac overnight." Adams and friends are building a forty-bed hospital that will include as a part of its therapy music, theater, and ceramics. "Our hospital will have secret passageways, slides, and interconnecting tree houses," he told us.

While some eccentrics are specialists, focusing all their nonconformity on a single, overriding obsession, we found that a surprisingly large number express their eccentricity in several different directions, which often seem to have little or no connection. Gary Holloway, an environmental planner working for the city of San Francisco, keeps a veritable stable of hobbyhorses. He is fascinated by Martin Van Buren, the eighth president of the United States. Eighteen years ago, he discovered that Van Buren was the only president not to have a society dedicated to his memory, so he promptly founded the Martin Van Buren Fan Club. "This man did absolutely nothing to further the course of our national destiny," Holloway told us proudly, "yet hundreds of people now follow me in commemorating him."

Holloway has served as the club's president for eighteen consecutive terms, and he has also been the winner for eighteen consecutive years of the Marty, its award for excellence in Van Burenism. Holloway is also a lifelong devotee of St. Francis of Assisi, and frequently dresses in the habit of a Franciscan monk. "It's comfortable, fun to wear, and I like the response I get when I wear it," he explained. "People always offer me a seat on the bus."

Holloway has an obsession with the British Commonwealth and has an encyclopedic knowledge of places such as Tristan da Cunha and Fiji. During the Falklands war he passionately espoused the cause of the islanders, to the point of flying the Falklands flag on the flagpole on his front lawn. After the war he celebrated Britain's victory by renaming his home Falklands House, where he continues to fly its flag. His bedroom at Falklands House still has everything in it that it had when he was a boy. He calls it the Peanuts Room because of his huge collection of stuffed Snoopies and other memorabilia pertaining to the comic strip *Peanuts*. He has slept on the same twin bed there for forty years. He has dozens of toy airplanes, relics of his boyhood, and the walls are covered with pennants. "As a monk," he explained, "I'm always doing pennants"—thereby demonstrating the sly sense of humor that many eccentrics possess.

The question of how best to measure intelligence is a vexed issue, and to treat it at any length would be an unnecessary digression for a book such as this. Suffice it to say that because of their very nature intelligence tests can measure only problem-solving abilities—convergent intelligence—and overlook divergent intelligence, the ability to formulate the problem. Some very great minds are simply bored by the notion of answering useless, hypothetical questions, and ordinary IQ tests are ineffectual in measuring their intelligence.

Nonetheless, standard IQ tests were a part of our procedure with all the subjects in the eccentrics project, and the results supported our *a priori* assumption that eccentrics tend to be above average in intelligence. The sample had an average IQ in the 115–120 range, more than one standard deviation above the norm; this places them in the top 10–15 percent of the population. However, it ought not to be taken too seriously, for while there are many extremely intelligent eccentrics, a great many possess only normal mental capacity; on the other hand, it is equally possible that eccentrics as a group are even more significantly intelligent than the results of the IQ tests suggested.

The other characteristics we found were incidental and anecdotal, usually relating directly to the individual's eccentricity. For example, we noticed that many of our subjects were bad spellers, but it was often a deliberate choice they had made: it wasn't that they didn't know how the dictionary spelled a word, but rather that, like Joyce and Faulkner, they preferred their own version. And while it is true to say that many eccentrics are unusual in their eating, sleeping, and living arrangements, it is especially true of those whose eccentricity is best expressed in those ways. However, the majority of the eccentrics in our study live in ordinary houses and have quite normal diets.

The one quality that seems to be universal among eccentrics is not on our list, because it is so subjective as to be incapable of being proved or disproved, yet it may be the most important: eccentrics appear to be happier than the rest of us. That is not to say that they are happy all the time; that would be a symptom of delusional madness, if not actual stupidity. But nearly everyone we met seemed to be pretty contented with his lot in life. Almost all of them exuded a sense of being comfortable with who they were. They were aware of the fact that many people found them strange, but it didn't bother them.

We have asserted that it is not scientific to discuss something without defining it objectively. Nonetheless, any discussion of happiness, particularly when it is observed in other people, obliges us to fall back on the familiar formula that although we cannot prove its existence logically, or even say precisely what it is, we know it when we see it. Time and again, the eccentrics in our study clearly evinced that shining sense of positivism and buoyant self-confidence that comes from being comfortable in one's own skin. We were always telling ourselves that if we could extract that happy essence and bottle it, we would be millionaires.

TWO

Four Hundred Years of Eccentrics

The past is a foreign country; they do things differently there.

—*L. P. Hartley,* The Go-Between

HISTORY IS WELL POPULATED WITH PEOPLE WHO WERE CELEBRATED for their quixotries and quiddities. While our study of living eccentrics was going on, we scoured the record for accounts of eccentrics of the past. In the case of someone like Emperor Norton, who lived in the not very remote past and who was renowned in his lifetime, there is a wealth of reasonably trustworthy eyewitness reports that permits us confidently to identify him as an eccentric. Even if the vocabulary is dated and arch—the emperor's contemporaries were apt to call him a "character" or a "quaint gentleman"—it is nonetheless abundantly clear that Norton would have been a star in our study.

However, the farther back one travels in time, the more

40

difficult it is to make a positive identification of eccentricity, because so many confounding factors become raveled together: eccentricity, madness, the superstitious fear of witches and demons, and senility all become blurred and confused. If L. P. Hartley was right, we might add that the farther back we go, the more exotic the past becomes. Once again we encounter problems in establishing parameters for normal behavior.

Where no reliable contemporary observations are available, we can get some clue as to the enormous variety in acceptable behaviors throughout history by looking at the legal codes, which have always been intended to establish the bare minimum of what was expected from the ordinary person. For example, it was a crime in Viking Iceland to write poetry about someone else, even if it was complimentary, but only if the verses exceeded four lines. The English peasant of the fourteenth century was not permitted by law to own a dog or send his son to school. All of the following have at different times been crimes in Britain: printing a book, professing the concept that blood circulates through the body, keeping gold at home, and buying goods on the way to market in order to make a profit. In seventeenth-century Salem, Massachusetts, the behavioral norm in one notorious period was mass hysteria; anyone who maintained the barest semblance of moderation and humanity was nonconforming.

Eccentricity has doubtless been with us in some form since the beginning of history: establish a norm anywhere, anytime, and there will be someone to flout it. However, the documentary sources we have from antiquity and the Middle Ages are so profoundly compromised as to be almost worthless. Was Nero really the madman that ax-grinding historians such as Tacitus have made him out to be? Or an artistic, misunderstood eccentric? We shall never know the answer, for the evidence is so scanty and so hopelessly conflicting. We decided that for our purposes there was little point in considering individuals who were known only from reports predating the first, rudimentary scientific thinking about the mind and the emergence of the concept of the personality. Further complicating matters is the fact that superstition was more prevalent in the remote past than it is now. Even in the early nineteenth century, the concept of eccentricity was fairly all-encompassing, including physical abnormalities, extreme longevity, and people who survived freak accidents. Dame Edith Sitwell is guilty of the same vagaries in *English Eccentrics,* published in 1933, which stirs in irrelevancies such as quacks and ornamental hermits, who were paid to behave as they did.

Our historical analysis covers the four hundred years from 1551 through 1950 and comprises 150 eccentrics, drawn from a wide variety of archival sources: legal documents, parish church records, the annals of local historical societies, and old newspapers, magazines, and encyclopedias. We included everyone we could turn up who was called eccentric (or any of the dozens of synonyms that have been in use over the years) by his contemporaries, which we were able to cross-verify in at least two independent sources. The earliest examples are all British. Frontier life in America was hard, and there was little place in it for eccentricity until the end of the eighteenth century. After the establishment of the republic, American eccentricity began to catch up with that of the mother country.

The earliest person we encountered whom we could with any confidence identify as an eccentric in the sense that we are using the word was the Hon. Henry Hastings, an English gentleman who was born in 1551. He delighted in hunting, fishing, and chasing women, and lived to be ninety-nine years old. He may have been the model for Sir Roger de Coverley, Addison and Steele's simple country squire. Hastings was always dressed in an old green suit and lived in an untidy house with cats, dogs, and tame hawks. He used the pulpit of a neighboring chapel as his larder, which he always kept well stocked with venison. One contemporary source described him as "an original in the age in which he lived, or rather he was the copy of our ancient nobility in hunting and warlike times." Hastings was still hunting and wenching at the age of ninety; he attributed his prodigious virility to a diet of oysters, which he ate twice a day.

Another Elizabethan eccentric was Lady Margaret Lambourne, who was so upset by the beheading of Mary, Queen of Scots, that, working alone, she plotted the assassination of Queen Elizabeth, who had ordered Mary's death. Lady Lambourne sneaked into the court dressed as a man and with two muskets concealed on her person—one for use on the queen, and the other for herself. But while she was stalking Elizabeth, who was walking in the garden, one of the muskets fell down and clattered on the flagstones, and she was seized.

When the queen confronted her, Lady Lambourne was

unrepentant, declaring that she had been moved to her desperate act by love. Elizabeth replied, "You have done your duty; now what do you think my duty is?"

Lady Lambourne immediately answered, "It depends on whether you are in the position of queen or judge."

Elizabeth replied that, in this instance, she acted as queen.

"You must therefore pardon me," said Lady Lambourne.

The queen, astounded, asked for an assurance that she would make no more attempts on her life.

"Madam," said Lady Lambourne, "a favor given under such restraints is no longer a favor, and in so doing Your Majesty would act against me as judge."

Elizabeth turned to her counselors and declared, "I have been thirty years a queen, but I do not remember ever having had a lecture read to me before." She granted Margaret Lambourne an unqualified pardon and safe conduct out of England.

The story has the unmistakable odor of legend, and it most likely survived because it portrays the queen in a benevolent light. Nonetheless, in Lady Lambourne's cracked logic—why should Elizabeth have to choose between those two particular alternatives, queen or judge?—we hear an authentic eccentric voice.

The English Civil War produced eccentrics on both sides. John Bigg (1629–96) was a wealthy scholar who acted as private secretary to one of the judges who passed the death sentence on Charles I. When the monarchy was restored and Charles II took the throne, Bigg withdrew from the world in disdain. For more than thirty years he lived in complete seclusion, known as the Hermit of Dinton. His principal occupation during the latter part of his life, it seems, was covering his clothes and shoes with thousands of tattered bits of leather.

The Royalist side produced Sir Thomas Urquhart (1611–60), the Scottish polymath, celebrated for his bizarre, extravagant use of language. His translation of Rabelais is still considered by many to be the best version in English. Taken prisoner at Worcester during the Civil War, Urquhart was imprisoned in the Tower of London. While he was in prison he wrote a book called *Peculiar Promptuary of Time,* which was intended to prove to Cromwell that he, Urquhart, was directly descended from Adam, in the hope of saving his neck from the Puritan's executioners. In his pedigree, Urquhart claimed to be 153rd in descent from Adam on his father's side, while on his mother's side he was 147th in descent from Eve.

Urquhart's prose style was the intoxicated apogee of the baroque in English, marked by sprawling structural complexity and a penchant for endless word catalogues, à la Rabelais. Here is a fine instance of his prose, from *The Jewel,* a panegyric to the Scots nation, in which he apologizes to the reader for the meagerness of his style, compared with what he might have written. Only a long extract does him justice.

I could truly have enlarged this discourse with a choicer variety of phrase, and made it overflow the field of the reader's understanding with an inundation of greater eloquence; and that one way, tropologetically, by metonymical, ironical, metaphorical, and synecdochical instruments of elocution, in all their several kinds, artificially effected, according to the nature of the subject, with emphatical expressions in things of greater concernment, with catachrestical in matters of meaner moment; attended on each side respectively with an epiplectic and exegetic modification; with hyperbolical, either epitatically or hypocoristically, as the purpose required to be elated or extenuated, with qualifying metaphors, and accompanied by apostrophes; and lastly, with allegories of all sorts, whether apologal, affabulatory, parabolary, aenigmatic, or paraemial. And on the other part, schematologetically adorning the proposed theme with the most especial and chief flowers of the garden of rhetoric and omitting no figure either of diction or sentence, that might contribute to the ear's enchantment, or persuasion of the hearer. I could have introduced, in case of obscurity, synonymal, exargastic, and palilogetic elucidations; for sweetness of phrase, antimetathetic commutations of epithets; for the vehement excitation of a matter, exclamation in the front and epiphonemas in the rear. I could have used, for the promptlier stirring up of passion, apostrophal and prosopopoeial diversions; and, for the appeasing and settling of them, some epanorthotic revocations, and aposiopetic restraints. I could have inserted dialogisms, displaying their interrogatory part with communicatively psymatic and sustenative flourishes; or proleptically, with the refutative schemes of anticipation and subjection, and that part which concerns the responsary, with the figures of permission and concession. Speeches extending a matter beyond what is, auxetically, digressively, transitiously, by ratiocination, aetiology, circumlocution, and other ways, I could have made use of; as likewise with words diminishing the worth of a thing, tapinotically, periphrastically, by rejection, translation, and other means, I could have served myself.

Another of Urquhart's grandiose projects was his *Logopandecteision,* a proposal for a universal language. As befits a language invented by an eccentric, it was exquisitely complex, with twelve parts of speech. Verbs would have four voices, seven moods, and eleven tenses; nouns and pronouns would have eleven cases, four numbers (singular, plural, dual, and redual), and eleven genders, "wherein," he assures the reader, "it exceedeth all other languages." Anticipating the wordplay of James Joyce, another eccentric writer, Urquhart claims that "every word in this language signifieth as well backward and forward, and however you invert the letter, still shall you fall upon significant words."

Urquhart's life ended in exile in France. According to tradition, he died of laughter when he heard about the restoration of the monarchy.

Our research revealed a great outburst of eccentricity beginning around 1725, with a peak in numbers during the last quarter of the eighteenth century. It is tempting to speculate about the possible connection between this flowering of nonconformity and the revolutionary political philosophies that were then emerging, but there were few eccentrics directly involved in the new free-thinking ideologies. Some of them came under the sway of Jean-Jacques Rousseau's romantic idealism, and several others could be considered to anticipate American-style democrats. However, the majority of eccentrics at this time were conservative to the point of xenophobia, and many more were politically naive to an extreme extent. Some of the new aristocracy and landed gentry were called eccentric by the old aristocrats, simply because they couldn't understand them or because they thought they were vulgar social climbers.

Some people regarded as eccentrics in the eighteenth century were in fact suffering from disorders that today would be recognized as mental illness; several were shown during their lifetime to be insane. Lord George Gordon (1751–93), the anti-Catholic rabble-rouser who led riots in London and was tried for treason, was subsequently diagnosed as mentally ill. At the end of his life, in exile in France, he embraced Judaism and changed his name to Israel Abraham George Gordon. Before her marriage, the Duchess of Queensberry (1703–77), wife of Charles, third Duke of Queensberry, was confined in a straitjacket, and her illness continued into her married life. Nevertheless, like Lord Gordon she has been included in many works dealing with historical eccentrics.

Since we are still not precise in distinguishing between eccentricity and mental illness at the end of the twentieth century, it is hardly surprising that people were confused about it in earlier periods. In the seventeenth century, when the insane were incarcerated in madhouses, the mentally ill of the middle and upper classes, whenever it was possible, were allowed to stay at home and potter about harmlessly. And the reverse situation may well have obtained: in our own time, there have certainly been cases where sane people were confined to institutions for the mentally ill. Is it possible that some of the inmates of such institutions in the past were really guilty of nothing more than eccentric behavior?

In the late eighteenth century, the Prince of Palagonia, Sicily, a shy man afraid of everyone, was thought mad simply because he had devoted his life to the study of monsters and chimeras. The interior of his house was filled with statues, mirrors, and surrealistic pyramids of cups, bowls, and saucers cemented together. The windows were full of colored glass, and his bedroom, populated by marble statues of many different kinds of animals, was called a Noah's Ark. The prince had surrounded his house with six hundred statues of imaginary creatures, some of them so hideous that the local authorities wanted to destroy them. They relented when they realized that to do so would break the prince's heart.

Some eccentrics of the past were mistaken for escaped mental patients. Sir Thomas Barrett-Lennard (1826–1919) was always shabbily dressed and continually misidentified as a gardener or servant. On one occasion, while returning from a meeting of the local asylum committee, which he chaired, he was mistaken for a patient and peremptorily detained against his will.

Our research revealed that the aristocracy and the landed gentry in Britain, as one might expect, had many more eccentrics among their number than did the lower classes. Dukes, countesses, churchmen, and wealthy landowners did indeed have their exploits well documented, but it was the members of the upper middle class who were preponderant:

TABLE 2.1:

Social Class Distribution of Historical Sample

Aristocracy	16%
Landed gentry	21%
Upper Middle Class	49%
Lower Middle Class	10%
Working Class	4%

We ought not to make too much of these figures; our archival sources were far more likely to report on the doings of the rich and noble than the poor and obscure. Yet it is nonetheless true that eccentric behavior has always been more frequent among the leisured classes, for eccentricity itself is essentially a leisure activity. Some eccentricities require money to be maintained, and a person who must hold down a job in order to put food on the table is not in a good position to tell the world to go to the devil.

William Beckford (1760–1844), visionary builder, collector, and author of the oriental tale *Vathek,* was heir to what was reputed to be the largest fortune in England. His childhood was gilded: he received music lessons from Mozart when he was five years old, and when he was seventeen published his first book, a wicked parody of the sententious handbooks that were given to people visiting stately homes such as the one he grew up in. His grand tour was conspicuously lavish, resembling a royal progress more than the finishing of a young man's education. He was received by Voltaire, and went out of his way at Naples to meet Farinelli, the great castrato. The singer was then in his seventies, but in his youth he had sung the same four tunes night after night for nearly twenty years to Philip V, the mad, insomniac king of Spain. Beckford wrote that the old man was so moved by "the remembrance of a period when he was almost deified" that he burst into tears. According to one of Beckford's biographers, the young man composed a Sicilian air on the spot to cheer him up.

Soon after his return to England his life was ruined by scandal, when he fell madly in love with a boy eight years his junior, the Hon. William Courtenay, later ninth Earl of Devon. In 1784 Beckford was caught *in flagrante* with the young noble by his tutor. Sodomy at that time was a capital crime, and so Beckford fled into self-imposed exile on the Continent. When he returned to England, he took up tower-building. Throughout the rest of his long life he was ostracized, and his frenzied, grandiose building projects may be interpreted as an attempt to establish a little world of his own, as well as a gesture of defiance to the world beyond.

He began small, with some romantic ruins and a mock abbey on the grounds of his vast estate near Hindon, Wiltshire. Then he grew bored with the augustan proportions of the immense Palladian mansion his father had left him, and he and his architect, James Wyatt, began the construction of Fonthill Abbey, a vast, fantastical creation that has an important place in English architectural history as one of the earliest major works of the Gothic Revival. Fonthill's first tower was made with shoddy materials, and a spring gale in 1797 brought it crashing to the ground. Beckford was undeterred and, with typical eccentric positivism, converted this setback into an opportunity to make the design even more grandiose. The new tower reached a height of 276 feet, making it one of the tallest buildings in England, visible for many miles around. Although he never succeeded in rehabilitating his reputation, Beckford's creation was one of the wonders of the age, considered by all who saw it to be incomparably sublime. Constable, who was generally hostile to the landed gentry, loved Fonthill Abbey, calling it "a romantic place, quite fairy land."

In 1825, a quarter of a century after its completion, the great tower collapsed. It is said that Beckford, who had long since moved to Bath (where he built a more sensible monument, Lansdown Tower, which has survived), saw it fall while sitting in his garden, nearly thirty miles away. If William Beckford was not a happy man, it was because he was a victim of social opprobrium on account of his illicit sexual preference; yet his natural disposition, according to those who knew him well, was witty and buoyant. But like most eccentrics, he was very much aware of how different he was. He once wrote of himself, "How strange my make-up is! The workings of my brain is enough to perplex anyone wanting to know about the composition of the human spirit!"

The landed gentry of England produced another eccentric in the melancholy strain, George Selwyn of Gloucestershire (1719–91). He was expelled from Oxford after he performed a blasphemous travesty of the Eucharist in his rooms. Famed as a wit and a wastrel, Selwyn was fascinated to an extreme degree by crime, death, and executions. His great friend Horace Walpole wrote that a lady of Selwyn's acquaintance once rebuked him as a barbarian for going to see a criminal being beheaded. Selwyn replied with aplomb, "If that was such a crime, I am sure I have made amends, for I went to see it sewed on again." Selwyn's macabre obsession was legendary; when Lord Holland lay on his sickbed, presumed to be dying, he told his servant, "The next time Mr. Selwyn calls, show him up: if I am alive I shall be delighted to see him, and if I am dead he will be glad to see me."

Eccentricity has never been, however, exclusively the purview of the high and mighty. One historical eccentric who could not lay claim to any sort of noble pedigree was a peddler from Edinburgh named Henry Prentice, who is reputed to have been the first man in Scotland to cultivate potatoes on a large scale. To his peers he was famed as a "great curio," and he was said never to have shaken the hand of anyone over the age of two. Having given most of his money away to poorhouses, he negotiated the purchase of a good resting place for himself in one of the better graveyards of Edinburgh. He demanded that the undertaker mount a lavish funeral procession for him, with a hearse and four coaches, and erected a monument in the grave-yard with this pithy inscription:

> Be not anxious how I lived,
> But rather how you yourself should die.

By the end of the eighteenth century, eccentricity had begun to make its appearance in America. Several of the young nation's founders exhibited behavior that bordered on the eccentric. Benjamin Franklin, for example, was a part-time nudist, a habit that probably originated in one of his thought experiments.

The strangest of all the early American heroes was John Chapman (1774–1845), better known as Johnny Appleseed. If anyone ever exemplified the eccentric trait of obsessive single-mindedness, it was he: he devoted his whole life to the apple, traveling across the country planting countless thousands or millions of apple trees over an area of land estimated to exceed 100,000 square miles. One pioneer who encountered him as he was walking through the Pennsylvania countryside, broadcasting appleseed, described him as "wiry, with long, dark hair and a scanty beard that was never shaved, and keen black eyes that sparkled with a peculiar brightness." He dressed in old coffee sacks with holes cut out for his arms and legs, and went barefoot except in the extreme cold.

Born near Springfield, Massachusetts, Johnny Appleseed was revered by all who met him, particularly the Indians, who believed that he was guided by holy spirits. The one thing that could ruffle his placid demeanor was to hear any slanderous reference made to the apple in the Garden of Eden. "That's wrong!" he would cry. "Look in the Good Book and you'll see that it says that they ate of 'the fruit of the tree.' Now that could be anything—a peach, a plum, a persimmon, a lemon—anything, in short, except an apple. Be sure the Lord wouldn't keep anyone from eating an apple. How many times is the apple mentioned in a favorable way in the Good Book? Eleven times, that's how many!"

ECCENTRICS

Davy Crockett, another American frontier hero, was always described as an eccentric by his contemporaries. A nurse at the Alamo described him thus: "He was the strangest man I ever saw. He had the face of a woman, and his manner was that of a girl. I could never regard him as a hero until I saw him die. He looked grand and terrible, shouting at the front door and fighting a whole column of Mexican infantry."

Although eccentricity is a phenomenon that affects both men and women, male eccentrics have been more widely recorded than their female counterparts, with about nine men eccentrics for every woman in the historical sample, though that statistic doubtless tells us more about the prejudice of the times than it does about the actual incidence of eccentricity, for men were far more likely to be mentioned in the archival sources. The males, who demonstrated greater variability in their behavior, came from all walks of life—earls, tinkers, high-court judges, and professional hermits. Female eccentrics, on the other hand, were almost exclusively from the upper classes and were primarily extroverts. They tended to be exceedingly outrageous and bizarre, and though they typically lived to advanced old age the passage of years did not diminish their eccentric habits. As we move forward through time, however, female eccentrics become less and less frequent. If more modern sources can be trusted, they had all but disappeared by the turn of this century, but in the 1920s they came roaring back with the onset of the renascence of eccentricity chronicled in this book.

Victoria Claflin Woodhull (1838–1927) was the most

glamorous and scandalous of the nineteenth-century American feminists, an advocate of free love and the first woman candidate for president. In an address in 1871, she claimed for herself and all women "an inalienable, constitutional, and natural right to love whom I may, to love as long or as short a period as I can, to change that love every day if I please!" She and her sister Tennessee (who later spelled it "Tennie C.") were born in Homer, Ohio, to a family that one biographer called "trash." Their parents, Buck and Roxy Claflin, put the girls on tour, first as a spiritualist act, giving public séances, and later in a medicine show peddling an "elixir of life." They landed in New York, where Tennessee gained the confidence of the elderly, ailing millionaire Colonel Cornelius Vanderbilt, who had great faith in her mesmeric healing powers. His family managed to prevent him from marrying the young adventuress, but he gave the two sisters a large sum of cash. They parlayed this money into a small fortune, which they used to establish *Woodhull & Claflin's Weekly,* a gossipy magazine devoted to spiritualism, free love, and Victoria Claflin Woodhull's presidential aspirations.

The magazine was a fun read and quite popular. One contemporary wrote that "*Woodhull & Claflin's Weekly* has voices from the 'seventh heaven,' and gabblings from a frog-pond . . . yet the amazing journal is crowded with thought, and with needed information that can be got nowhere else." It was in the pages of this journal that Victoria Woodhull launched one of the greatest scandals in American history, accusing Henry Ward Beecher, the powerful abolitionist preacher, of adultery. While most eccentrics tend to become even more nonconforming in later life, the Claflin sisters, their spirit perhaps broken by the widespread malicious publicity about them during the Beecher affair, finished their long lives quietly: they both married English millionaires (Tennessee's was a baronet).

Another woman eccentric with an *idée fixe* was Lady Margaret-Ann Tyrrell (1870–1939), the wife of a British diplomat, whose lifework was the composition of a new kind of parallel history, simultaneously tracing events in all parts of the world from 2000 B.C. to modern times. With so many threads to research, annotate, and cross-reference, it was little wonder that Lady Tyrrell was prone to forgetfulness and social gaffes, such as mistaking the future George VI for her husband's private secretary. During her husband's diplomatic posting to Paris, she preferred to avoid official functions altogether, and sat ensconced in the uppermost branches of a tree in the embassy gardens, where she scribbled away at her history.

The stereotype of the eccentric woman is an old lady in a big house with a hundred cats; we turned up one eccentric, Susanna Kennedy, countess of Eglintoune, who preferred rats. One of the greatest beauties of the eighteenth century, she complained at the end of her long life (she lived to be ninety-one) of never having received true gratitude from anyone other than four-footed animals. She kept hundreds of rats, summoning them to the dining room at mealtimes by tapping on an oak panel. At this cue, a dozen of her favorites would appear out of the woodwork and join her at the table. After dinner, at a quiet word of command, the rats would retire in an orderly fashion.

The stereotype of the male eccentric, the absent-minded professor, turned out to be well founded in fact. Scholarly circles have historically been a fertile breeding ground for the eccentric way of life. Samuel Johnson, for instance, was not only a prodigy of wit, erudition, and courage, but also a whimsical man who delighted in rolling down steep hills to amuse his friends. Most scholarly eccentrics tended to be shy, quiet, and introverted. Some of them had difficulty in coping with the ordinary activities of daily life, even to the point of being unable to communicate. John Barrett (1753–1821), a classicist at Trinity College, Dublin, spoke Latin and Greek fluently, but his English was said to be appallingly bad. Another such a one was Thomas Spooner (1844–1930), dean and warden of New College, Oxford. A near-blind albino, Spooner will always be remembered for the verbal tic named after him. A spoonerism is the transposition, accidental or otherwise, of the initial sounds of words, usually with ludicrous results. Thus "We all know what it is to have a half-warmed fish within us" (for "half-formed wish"); or "The Lord is a shoving leopard."

Throughout history, eccentrics have been regarded by their contemporaries in many different ways, and we found it difficult to make a meaningful assessment of the personality traits of the historical eccentrics from the yellowing pages of our primary sources. Only broad sweeps of the brush were possible: the best we could hope for was to discriminate between introversion and extroversion. Those who were extrovert in character tended to be well liked, outgoing, and popular (though somewhat impulsive), and despite everything held in high esteem by their friends.

Introverts, on the other hand, had fewer friends and were often treated with suspicion.

We concluded that recluses might be presumed to be introverts unless there was evidence to the contrary. Independent descriptions by several contemporary witnesses reinforced the personality assessments, though the evidence was sometimes apparently contradictory. Here, in the case of Henry Lee Warner (1722–1802), is positive evidence of extroversion, in a description by one of his contemporaries: "Well liked by many. He is a truly amiable man. He is too good. He has an extreme tenderness of disposition." Yet there was also some evidence that he was an intellectual introvert. He slept all day so as to concentrate on his scholarly inquiries into the natural sciences without interruption by night. He came to be known as "England's nicest man." Thus his curious attire—the gold-laced coat, silk neck-cloth, and curved-toed shoes of the previous century—went largely unnoticed.

Using such biographical clues, we deduced that roughly three-quarters of the historical sample could be seen as mainly extrovert, and the remaining quarter as introvert. The evidence for some of these descriptions was admittedly slender, sometimes based upon a single word, such as "taciturn," "surly," or "piquant." However, it is possible that the preponderance of extroverts in the historical sample is due to the fact that they are simply more newsworthy; journalists have never been interested in writing about quiet people leading quiet lives.

Some great eccentrics broke every standard of accepted behavior, making them famous in their lifetimes, even though their underlying motivation remains mysterious. One such person was Jack Mytton, one of the most notorious hell-raisers of all time, whose life, understandably, was not a long one (1796–1834). Expelled from both Westminster School and Harrow for fighting, he gave away money and spent about half a million pounds on alcohol in seventeen years. Port was his favorite drink, at the rate of five bottles a day, but in a pinch eau de cologne or lavender water would do. His wardrobe contained 150 pairs of riding breeches, 700 pairs of boots, more than 1,000 hats, and nearly 3,000 shirts.

A daredevil sportsman, what Mytton really enjoyed was risking his life. Fear was not in his nature. He became so famous for taking equestrian jumps no one else would contemplate that a phrase was coined to describe anything too tough to attempt—"It would do for Mytton." He scorned caution and wondered why others did not do likewise. When a friend, visibly shaky as he rode next to him in his gig, confided that he had never been in a crash, Mytton was shocked. "What ho!" cried Mytton. "Never, you say? What a damned slow fellow you must have been all your life!" Then he promptly drove the carriage over the bank and overturned it.

Havoc broke loose at one of Mytton's dinner parties, when he appeared in full hunting costume, mounted on his bear, Nell. In the ensuing panic, while his friends jumped out of windows or clambered behind chairs, Mytton called out "Tally-ho" and spurred his mount, which turned impatient and ate part of his leg. Many anecdotes attest to his love of animals; at one point he had some two thousand dogs, which he fed champagne and steak. He also kept sixty cats, some of which he dressed in livery.

Mytton's penchant for self-destruction finally got the better of him, when he set himself on fire to cure a bad case of the hiccups. Although burned to the bone, he is said to have exulted, "Well, the hiccup is gone, by God!" One version of the story has it that he died as a result of the burns, another that he survived and dined the next day with a friend, swathed in bandages like a mummy.

The strain of eccentricity that produced mad lords and landed gentry such as Jack Mytton is expressed in America in a long line of eccentric millionaires, of which Howard Hughes is the final, crowning glory. At the mild end of the spectrum are the practitioners of extreme ostentation, such as James "Silver Dollar" West (1903–57), a Texas oil millionaire who used to fling silver dollars from the window of his hotel room in Houston to pedestrians below. Palm Beach, Florida, is one of the horsiest places on earth, but Cornelius K. G. "Horseback" Billings (1861–1931) took it to an extreme: to celebrate the opening of his new stable, he arranged an outdoor dinner at which the guests, formally attired, came mounted on their horses. This party was such a great success that he repeated it at Louis Sherry's posh restaurant in New York City. The guests, again mounted on horseback, were conveyed to the dining room on the elevator and dined on pheasants from feed bags, washed down by rivers of vintage champagne.

True eccentrics are never acting. They are strong individuals with strange inclinations of their own, which they are not afraid to express. They repudiate nothing. They refuse to compromise. Even though we were only able to encounter these eccentrics of the past through the eyes of their contemporaries, who were often prudish, unimaginative, or unsympathetic for reasons that we now find difficult to understand, time and again we could discern in their lives the same happy sense of personal liberty that we were discovering in our interviews with the living eccentrics.

THREE

Eccentricity and Creativity: The Artists

Life should be a perpetual Kyrie eleison: instead of which it
is only a chorus of Offenbach's.

—*Ouida, letter, c. 1895*

IF WE ACCEPT THAT A HIGH PROPORTION OF THE EXTREMELY GIFTED
are eccentric, is it a valid corollary, then, that an equally
high proportion of eccentrics are creative? The study allowed us to try to answer that question at first hand. Three-
quarters of the eccentric sample described themselves as
creative, and almost that many believed themselves to be
original—numbers that proved not to be exaggerations. We
found that the eccentrics in our sample were an extraordinarily ingenious group of people, expressing themselves
in every conceivable medium.

Two main groups emerged, the artists and the scientists,
with a third, smaller group of religious eccentrics. The first
group comprised poets and novelists, painters and sculp-

tors, filmmakers and architects, and craftsmen working in all sorts of unusual media. The scientists were mostly inventors; one of the religious eccentrics had founded his own religion, a modern version of nature worship, with the founder's girlfriend as high priestess.

Creativity was one point about which the eccentrics themselves had obviously thought a great deal. Several of them extrapolated from their own experiences and helped us to sharpen the issues. The following statement, from an eccentric forty-two-year-old philosopher named Hubert Craxton, shows an admirable grasp of a question at the heart of the matter:

> Are all creative people—artists, mystics and reformers, Jesus, Buddha, thinkers such as Wittgenstein, etc.—eccentrics? Are the traits of nonconformity essential for an individual to be a reformer or a creative individual? Are the truth and meaning in the writings of such philosophers, religious reformers and artists not really external, universal verities, as is so often assumed, but merely expressions of an eccentric attitude of mind? Could it be that these individuals do not in fact widen the limits of our own conceptual realities, but merely act out their own "karma" in their eccentric traits? Are they, in other words, not authentic, but merely charlatans, and are their insights irrelevant to the conformist, socially conditioned lifestyles of most people?

Craxton puts his finger on a central problem: all creative acts are by definition a departure from the established norm—which is a loose way of defining eccentricity. Dostoyevsky was getting at something close to this in the famous Grand Inquisitor episode of *The Brothers Karamazov:* if Jesus were to return to the world in modern times, he would be much too radical and strange—too eccentric, perhaps—for the church he founded.

Picasso and Stravinsky are known as great masters because they succeeded; most of the eccentric artists in our study have not yet found acceptance with critics or the public, and are therefore regarded as being simply batty. Yet when Picasso and Stravinsky pioneered their revolutionary styles, they, too, were widely criticized for being willful, bizarre, extremist—again, words commonly used to describe the eccentric.

We have postulated that eccentricity is a continuum; it may be that it is impossible to be an artist of great originality and merit without tending toward the eccentric end of the spectrum. Probably neither Picasso nor Stravinsky would quite have qualified for the study, but they were both nonconforming to a significant degree. Without their pronounced individualism, they might never have achieved their outstanding artistic originality.

While there has been a great deal of psychological research and theorizing about creativity and the conditions it requires, the subject is still mysterious. Freud believed that creative people enjoyed "looseness of repression," a temporary removal of intellectual control that permitted them to make achievements of what he called "special perfection." A loosening of the normal reins of consciousness allows the creative person to act on unconscious impulses even in the face of opposition. According to Freud, the ability to stand up for one's convictions—and to act on one's whims—was more likely to be present in those who retained a childlike openness to new experiences: again, an apt description of the eccentric.

In the early years of the twentieth century, psychologists speculated that there were two complementary intellectual processes—dissociation and association, or analysis and synthesis—to explain the workings of the imagination. That distinction was based partly on the field observations of Richard Rothe, an art educator in Vienna. He distinguished two basic approaches to art: "The first type builds up his drawings or sculptures out of separate parts, as one would build with bricks. This is the 'building type,' in contrast to the 'seeing type,' who proceeds quite differently, by molding the form he is aiming at out of a single piece. He holds in his hand the piece of clay with which he is working, and turns it round and round while at work. While he is working, he thinks of a definite figure in a definite posture." It would be tempting to speculate that these approaches could represent more than stylistic preferences, and might rather be early orientations toward either inductive or deductive reasoning—intuition versus analysis.

In the twentieth century, other behavioral scientists, drawing on published accounts about high-powered inspiration in the past and direct observation of gifted individuals in the present, developed a more detailed analysis of the creative process. The American psychologist Brewster Ghiselin, in his book *The Creative Process,* published in 1952, advanced theories based on firsthand accounts of eminent artists and scientists such as William Faulkner,

Henry James, Katherine Mansfield, Henri Poincaré, Paul Va-
léry, and Alfred North Whitehead, among others. Ghiselin,
expanding on the earlier theories of Graham Wallas, set
forth four stages in the creative process: preparation, incubation, illumination, and verification.

In the preparation stage, the creator recognizes that a
problem requires solution, or that a particular idea or theme
is a fitting subject to be explored. This stage includes the
time in which the problem is being explored, during which
the creator works to develop the skills and knowledge necessary to solve it. Then there often follows an intervening
period of frustration, which becomes more acute when all
the obvious preparation and background research has been
done, but the solution is still elusive.

In the incubation period, the whole subject sinks into the
subconscious, but the mind continues to work upon it in
mysterious and poorly understood ways. For the artist, this
stage typically involves trial-and-error stylistic experimentation. Then, in the illumination stage, a solution abruptly
emerges into full consciousness. There is a great deal of
variability from field to field and from person to person as
to how each of these stages is reached. Finally, in the verification stage, the solution is put to the acid test. In the case
of creative science, empirical work is implemented to confirm the hypothesis; for the artist it is simply a matter of
presenting the work to friends and the public, and then
observing their reactions.

My own concept of creativity is that it is effective, em-
pathic problem-solving. The part that empathy plays in this
formulation is that it represents a transaction between the

individual and the problem. (I am using the word "problem" loosely, as did Ghiselin: for an artist the problem might be how to depict an apple.) The creative person displaces his point of view into the problem, investing it with something of his own intellect and personality, and even draws insights from it. He identifies himself with all the depths of the problem. Georges Braque expounded a version of this concept succinctly: "One must not just depict the objects, one must penetrate into them, and one must oneself become the object."

This total immersion in the problem means that there is a great commitment to understand it at all costs, a deep commitment that recognizes no limits. In some cases the behavior that results can appear extreme by everyday standards. For example, when the brilliant architect Kiyo Izumi was designing a hospital for schizophrenics, he took LSD, which mimics some of the effects of schizophrenia, in order to understand the perceptual distortions of the people who would be living in the building. This phenomenon of total immersion is typical of eccentricity: overboard is the only way most eccentrics know how to go.

Time and again, we find creativity being described in terms that are commonly used to define eccentricity. The theory of creativity outlined here assumes that it can be not only perceived but learned. After we had interviewed a large number of the eccentrics intensively, I found myself returning again and again to the question posed at the beginning of this chapter: if creative people are eccentric, then is it possible that eccentricity itself is a component of creativity? Perhaps if we knew more about the inner workings of the minds of creative eccentrics, it would be possible for normal people to model their thinking on the remarkable few who are prolifically original.

Peter McGough and David McDermott are artists who until recently lived simultaneously in two places: New York City of the late twentieth century and an idealized nineteenth-century American arcadia of their own devising. Their apartment on the Lower East Side of Manhattan and their studio, a turn-of-the-century bank in Williamsburg, Brooklyn, contained almost no objects made in this century. They covered the walls with Victorian portraits and other antique bric-a-brac they bought at flea markets and tag sales in upstate New York.

The two men wear only antique clothes, which are often near tatters. McDermott favors fancy Victorian silk neckcloths and a disreputable-looking beaver top hat, while McGough prefers a slightly more up-to-date costume. McDermott writes letters to his friends (including his pen pals in prison) on old paper with a quill pen. He pastes a canceled antique penny stamp on the front of the envelope, and correct modern postage is affixed to the back. The modern stamps can be peeled off, making the letter exactly resemble a message from the past—which is, in fact, what it is. "Little things like that are important," he said. McGough and McDermott's concept of time travel is explained in an essay in a book they published in 1990. The text was written by a former disciple, who styles himself Jeffrey Dean Gasperini, Gent.:

Time Travel is facilitated through the Aeſthetic Control of ones Domal Environment. The Accurate Decoration of a Period Interior, with consideration to its Historical Purpoſe becomes the Science. Upon entrance to the Phyſical Paſt is the Soul tranſported to the Spiritual Paſt, and the Vehicle of Conveyance, be it by Foot, Horſe, or Railway Car, becomes the Time Machine. . . . Habiliments of the Epoch catalyze the diſcarding of Modernity's Manneriſms to affect an Antique Demeanor: one's poſture is rendered Hiſtorical by the aids of a ſtarched Collar and padded Waiſtcoat. . . . He who is moſt cognizant of the Details of the Domicile ſhall be eſteemed the greatest Ambassador to "What Shall Come" through his affinity for "What Has Paſſed." We may well extend this idea of Time Travel beyond the Interior to the entire Houſe, Neighborhood, City, and Beyond! We envision the Day when whole Nations will experience the moſt Glorious Periods of their Hiſtory; when Roman Oarships, Spanish Galleons, and American Clipper Ships ſhall traverſe the Seas, all to return whence they iſſued to Harbor Villages of like Antiquity.

When McGough and McDermott moved their painting studio to Brooklyn, they rewired the bank building, ripping out the modern electrical wiring and replacing it with old-fashioned, cloth-wrapped wiring, complete with Edison-style tungsten bulbs. They call this expensive, time-consuming process "de-vinylizing." McDermott told us, "We want to get rid of all the modern things, and restore [the building] to the condition it was in when the ancestors were here. That's what we call the people who lived before—the ancestors."

The two men have put time travel at the center of their art. They first made their names in the art world with symbolic paintings in a naive style, which are frequently emblazoned with puzzling, vaguely moralistic slogans. Then they took up photography. Using a huge nineteenth-century camera, they dressed their clients in antique clothes and took their portraits in formal settings that mimicked those used by Victorian salon photographers. David McDermott told us that they had trouble finding assistants who were sympathetic to their unorthodox methods. He was horrified to find that one assistant was using a plastic basin to develop the film, and devoted several weeks to a search for an old-fashioned porcelain basin, which he finally found at a butcher supply shop.

Although McGough and McDermott lived and worked in dangerous neighborhoods, they were not afraid of being mugged. "Whenever bad guys look at us," McDermott told us, "we just wave our arms and shout 'God bless you! God bless you!' and they leave us alone."

One of the traits common to most eccentric artists is an extraordinarily vivid imagination. That might sound redundant—how good is an artist who lacks a vivid imagination?—but here we are referring to extremely intense, even involuntary, visual imagery, sometimes referred to in the past as visions. McGough and McDermott's vision of "Roman Oarships, Spanish Galleons, and American Clipper Ships," all sailing together in a glorious flotilla of an ideal past reincarnate, has that intense visual quality.

One of the subjects in the study, a thirty-three-year-old

eccentric named Ryan Parmenter, a master puppeteer, gave us this precise, vivid description of his mental images:

> My mind works in a series of patterns, a scheme of ideas. Stripping objects of their detail to give one picture. In order to recognize an object, the mind must have somewhere deep within itself a picture, an image. The mind is constantly sifting information and constantly analyzing the world into these patterns. The rate at which these patterns fall into place gives you a measure of human emotions. Two disparate images which are not normally put together are put together by the mind to produce a completely different idea. By doing so you experience a sensation of delight, a feeling that means something.

This theory of the visionary process, developed independently by an eccentric who relates it directly to a heightened emotional state, makes an important and original association between visual imagery and the creative process. Psychologists have hinted at this connection in the past, but no one has explored it thoroughly. As Parmenter suggests, an image is active, and it operates on concrete and abstract ideas within the mind. It creates new forms of information by means of synthesis, conceptual analysis, symbolism, and modeling.

A person's control over his imaging ability may also be an important key to creativity. As early as 1893, Sir Francis Galton noted that there was a tremendous range in the clarity, flexibility, and mastery people had over their mental images. Galton was something of an eccentric himself; a first cousin of Charles Darwin, he was a noted African explorer and meteorologist before he turned to the study of genetics. He once began to experiment on himself with drugs in alphabetical order, but he stopped at C, after castor oil had its usual effect. He patented a ventilating hat, which cooled the head by lifting automatically from time to time. Galton believed that genius was hereditary, and in 1869 he published a rambling monograph called *Hereditary Genius,* in which he traced the family trees of outstanding judges, statesmen, scientists, poets, musicians, painters, divines, oarsmen, and wrestlers, to prove that excellence in all fields is inherited.

In some cases, the eccentric's images are so vivid that they impair his ability to communicate. One of the eccentrics in our study is a novelist named Alex Stella, from Binghamton, New York, whose style is an ornate literary phantasmagoria reminiscent of that of Sir Thomas Urquhart. His visions are startlingly vivid, to the point of seeming exaggerated and even ridiculous. Here, for example, is the first paragraph of his novel *a younger earth:*

> Body swaying with the stream of sussurus and music, muffled but frenetic, issuing through the gilt-lattice trim doorway, the young woman mused on the tiny golden bubbles she pictured in a candle-lit glass of champagne. Robin imagined herself being gently buffeted out of the cool, beige liquid, naked and rising with those bubbles. In a twinkling, all sights, all sounds, all sensations had become pleasurable. She didn't have to strain to hear the rhythmic popping of the bubbles, to feel the warm air on her breast and belly, to taste

piquant champagne still clinging to her lips and look upon herself in delight.

Stella published *a younger earth* himself, after he was turned down by many prominent agents and publishers. On the novel's back cover there is a portrait of the author and a request to the reader to write a letter to Scott Meredith, a well-known literary agent, with the address of his office in New York. Meredith, obviously, wasn't pleased with this gratuitous invocation of his name, and lodged a legal protest against Stella. Thereafter the book now came with an insert that stated, "This copy of *a younger earth* is a collector's item," and went on to explain that Scott Meredith had nothing to do with the book. Stella concluded with a rare burst of realism:

> According to legal counsel, I should be very grateful that Mr. Meredith is disinclined to make mountains out of molehills. It happens I agree. And, if I may, I should like to conclude by rescinding my request to send Mr. Meredith letters or postcards. I profoundly doubt he would welcome receiving any. Anyway, I've learned he's patient and tolerant, but please let us not push it.

Just as Alex Stella's literary style is a bit too vivid, so his marketing strategy was too ingenious. Yet, with typical eccentric optimism, he provided several blank forms at the back of the book for readers to order additional copies.

Two contemporary British psychologists, Neil Durndell and A. E. Wetherick, conducted a study that found a direct correspondence between the subjects' control over their mental imagery and their scores on a psychometric test of creative thinking. This connection, too, was supported by comments from some of the eccentric subjects in our study:

> My imagination, and my control over it, is strong. I imagine anything, then ask, "What system could it be in? What are the linkages?" I then extend the logical possibilities for as far as they will go, and beyond, into darker, nefarious, subterranean areas. I do this best in a semisleeping, half-awake, slowed-up reverie, which I first found to be full of angst, frustration, and half-remembered ideas. Now I greet it expectantly, warmly: it sometimes comes out after lunch or at a concert, with my eyes closed, but this can't be planned. It's like the case of Salvador Dalí and his famous Camembert cheese. [Salvador Dalí used to eat large quantities of ripe Camembert cheese, in the belief that it made him dream more often, more vividly, and more weirdly, providing him with images that he transferred directly into his art.]
>
> —Matthew, age 42

> I can imagine a visual or sound effect, then work to create it. When I am reading, I can visualize, hear, feel, smell, in my imagination. Words stimulate my imagination as well as sounds and colors. I can see ahead and really anticipate consequences.
>
> —Sheila, age 52

> When my wife speaks of any place or event, I see it in color, vividly. I describe to her what I imagine, and she assures me that the picture is correct.
>
> —Sylvan, age 74

I can see faces, wraiths, shapes, forms, etc. in designs on wallpapers, carpets, and so forth. They stay in my mind after I shut my eyes, and sometimes after I have fallen asleep I see them in my dreams. Most times, this allows me to have an almost perfect photographic memory over long periods of time.

—Val, age 51

These accounts are typical of many descriptions we received from eccentrics who experience extremely vivid, detailed imagery, a phenomenon known to psychologists as eidetic imagery. Eidetic imagery is a way of mentally representing objects and events with a sparkling clarity that possesses all the sensorial characteristics of a real experience. It is closely related to the lay concept of the "photographic memory." This capacity is often well developed in young children but in most people, as they grow older and acquire a more abstract method of processing information, it gradually fades.

This childlike propensity of the creative mind was characteristic of Albert Einstein, one of the most visionary thinkers of the twentieth century, who had strong eccentric traits. He developed his theory of relativity using information that had been available to mathematicians for at least fifty years. When a friend asked him how he had conceived his theory, he replied, "The normal adult never bothers his head about space-time problems. Everything there is to be thought about, in his opinion, was already done in early childhood. I, on the contrary, developed so slowly that I only began to wonder about space and time when I was grown up. In consequence I probed deeper into the problem than an ordinary child would have done." At a banquet for his seventy-fourth birthday he declared, "Birthdays are for children, but why should I not, for once in my life, make an exception? I am only afraid that it will make such a stir that the ambassador from Mars will be present."

Another creative genius who was often described by his contemporaries as being childlike was William Blake. The intense vividness of his poetry and engravings resulted from the fact that they were, literally, visions, graphic revelations that intruded themselves from the outside onto his mind. Blake frequently called his works visions, and claimed that they were revealed to him by visiting spirits, like the angels who appeared to the Hebrew prophets. In 1819 he met an artist and astrologist named John Varley, with whom he held séances. Spirits would appear to them, and Blake would draw their portraits. One of them, "The Man Who Taught Blake Painting," was an ethereal-looking youth with enormous, crinkled eyes and a flamelike growth in the middle of his forehead. Varley wrote that there were sometimes so many spirits waiting for a turn that they would jostle one another in Blake's vision.

It would be dangerous to attempt a thoroughgoing psychoanalysis of Blake, for his poetry and designs are highly finished works of art, and thus controlled by the laws of aesthetics rather than those of psychology. It is at least unlikely that a man of his accomplishments, well liked by all who knew him, could have been suffering from schizophrenia or any other serious mental illness that causes hallucinations. That is not to say that we believe in ghostly visitations; rather, we simply do not have enough information to evaluate Blake's visions, and must take him on his own terms. Yet there can be no doubt that he did experience visions of one sort or another. Kenneth Clark offered one explanation in his classic treatise *The Nude:* "[Blake] had an exceptional power of secreting retinal images, and it was, to some extent, the unconscious memory of these images which he identified with inspiration. He was justified in saying that 'all forms are perfected in the poet's mind.' "

Blake himself wrote at great and eloquent length about his visionary beliefs, which are too complex to be discussed here. In his letters, however, we can come closer to the temper of the man than in his finished literary productions. A verse letter written on September 12, 1800, to John Flaxman, the sculptor with whom Blake later collaborated, reveals how vivid were his visions:

. . . Milton lov'd me in childhood & shew'd me his face.
Ezra came with Isaiah the Prophet, but Shakespeare in
     riper years gave me his hand;
Paracelcus & Behmen appear'd to me, terrors appear'd in
     the Heavens above
And in the Hell beneath, & a mighty & awful change
     threatened the Earth.
The American War began. All its dark horrors passed before
     my face
Across the Atlantic to France. Then the French

7 8

Revolution commenc'd in thick clouds,
And My Angels have told me that seeing such visions
I could not subsist on Earth,
But by my conjunction with Flaxman, who knows to
forgive Nervous Fear.

In a letter to a Rev. Trusler, written on August 23, 1799, Blake reveals the childlike positivism characteristic of eccentrics, using language that closely resembles some of the comments we heard from subjects in our study nearly two hundred years later:

Mirth is better than Fun, & Happiness is better than Mirth. I feel that a Man may be happy in This World. And I know that This World Is a World of imagination and Vision. I see Every thing I paint In This World, but Every body does not see alike. . . .

But I am happy to find a Great Majority of Fellow Mortals who can Elucidate My Visions, & Particularly they have been Elucidated by Children, who have taken a greater delight in contemplating my Pictures than I even hoped.

The preternatural intensity of Blake's visual imagery continually asserted itself. To his friend William Hayley he confided, "My wife is like a flame of many colours of precious jewels"; and he added, "My fingers Emit sparks of fire with Expectation of my future labours" (letter, September 16, 1800). Anecdotal evidence from contemporaries confirms that he lived the visions he wrote about. Once when a friend stopped by unannounced at his house in Lambeth, he found Blake and his wife sitting in the garden naked, reading *Paradise Lost* to each other aloud.

Architecture, the most impressive of the arts, has attracted some spectacular eccentric practitioners. Sarah Winchester, widow of the American arms manufacturer Oliver Winchester, believed that the ghosts of people killed by her husband's rifles would haunt her unless she built a magnificent house large enough to accommodate a legion of friendly ghosts to protect her. For thirty-eight years, the mansion in San Jose, California, continued to grow; a sort of architectural Scheherazade, Mrs. Winchester believed that she would live as long as she kept building.

By the time of her death in 1922, the house was eight stories tall, with 158 rooms (not counting the secret chambers), 2,000 doors, 10,000 windows, and 48 fireplaces. It is a bizarre place, filled with snares intended to thwart malicious spirits. One stairway has 44 steps and 7 turns in an ascent of less than 10 feet; some of the chimneys are false, to smoke out unwelcome phantoms. Mrs. Winchester built in an escape route for herself, an enormous bell tower inaccessible from outside, which gave access, by a rope, to a subterranean hideout.

Edward Leedskalnin (1887–1951) is another classic case of overdoing it: he built an immense castle entirely of coral, to impress the girl he loved. The Latvian immigrant singlehandedly quarried and moved into place thousands of tons of coral rock at his site in Florida City, Florida, where he built a gigantic monument to his passion. He carved an obelisk twenty-seven feet high. Bizarre sculptures and furniture are everywhere: rocking chairs, bathtubs, and a so-called "repentance corner," an object resembling a Puritan pillory. One door to his park weighs nine tons, but it is so well balanced that a child can easily open it.

One of the great English eccentrics of this century built his architectural fantasy in Mexico. Edward James (1907–84) is believed to have been the illegitimate son of Edward VII, which would make him the natural great-uncle of Queen Elizabeth II. A terrible poet, James gave away large sums of money to Salvador Dalí, René Magritte, and other surrealist artists, and assembled an impressive collection of their best works. In 1945 he bought several thousand acres of jungle in Xilitla, and built his outrageous dream palace, which he is said to have conceived under the influence of marijuana and psychedelic mushrooms. Suspended against a mountainside, it is a riotous fantasy composed of Greek columns that support nothing, bridges that lead nowhere, and round orange doors that don't open. Spiral staircases climb gracefully above flower-shaped fountains. James said of his work, "When archaeologists come and see this in two or three thousand years' time, they won't know what to make of it."

He was a tall, strange man with a long white beard that flowed over a peasant poncho. He walked with two sticks, to compensate for the limitations imposed by his immensely long, downward-curving toenails. He frequently strolled completely naked through the jungle around Xilitla, where he cultivated orchids and kept boa constrictors. The anthropologist Angel Castrillon wrote that James had a breakdown when he saw a peasant cutting down a plant with his machete: "James wept uncontrollably. He repeated over and over to the poor, confused man, 'You're an assassin! An assassin!' "

One story about James is almost too good to be true. It is said that when he was staying at the Majestic Hotel in Mexico City, he brought his snakes and the mice intended for their dinner. When a mouse escaped into the hallway, an American lady staying next door to James shrieked that the hotel was infested. The maid tried to calm her, saying, "Oh no, señora, they are not the hotel's mice. They are food for the gentleman's snakes, in the room next door."

Musicians, whose works exist in the realm of abstraction, have always been subject to flights of fancy. Erik Satie, whose compositions are spun from the gossamer of whimsy, exhibited a whole panoply of eccentric traits. He first came to prominence as a member of an occult society, the Rose + Croix, which was led by a mage named Josephin Peladan. A former bank clerk who called himself Sar, an ancient Babylonian name, Peladan wore a flowing violet robe with a silver waistcoat and lace cuffs. Satie wrote fanfares and incidental piano music for the cult's absurd pageants. Before long the composer's exquisite sense of the ridiculous got the better of him, and he resigned.

Satie always operated by a different set of rules from the rest of the world: in 1914 the publisher Lucien Vogel tried to commission Stravinsky to write music to accompany some drawings by Charles Martin, called *Sports et Divertissements*. Stravinsky refused because the fee was too small. Then the publisher approached Satie, who turned it down, although desperately poor, saying the fee was too high! When Vogel reduced the fee he accepted, and wrote one of his most successful piano suites. In a book called *The Memoirs of an Amnesiac,* Satie explained his working habits, in a *jeu d'esprit* called "The Musician's Day," as close as anything that exists to *The Eccentric's Handbook:*

An artist must organize his life.

Here is the exact timetable of my daily activities:

Get up: 7:18 A.M.; be inspired 10:23 to 11:47 A.M. I take lunch at 12:11 P.M. and leave the table at 12:14 P.M.

Healthy horse-riding, out in the grounds: 1:19 to 2:53 P.M. More inspiration: 3:12 to 4:07 P.M.

Various activities (fencing, reflection, immobility, visits, contemplation, swimming, etc. . . .): 4:21 to 6:47 P.M.

Dinner is served at 7:16 and ends at 7:20 P.M. Then comes symphonic readings, out loud: 8:09 to 9:59 P.M.

I go to bed regularly at 10:37 P.M. Once a week (on Tuesdays) I wake up with a start at 3:19 A.M.

I eat only white foods: eggs, sugar, scraped bones; fat from dead animals; veal, salt, coconuts, chicken cooked in white water; fruit mold, rice, turnips; camphorated black pudding, things like pasta, cheese (white), cotton salad, and certain fish (without skins).

I boil my wine and drink it cold mixed with fuchsia juice. I have a good appetite, but never talk while eating, for fear of strangling myself.

I breathe carefully (a little at a time). I very rarely dance. When I walk, I hold my sides and look rigidly behind me.

Serious in appearance, if I laugh it is not on purpose. I always apologize about it nicely.

My sleep is deep, but I keep one eye open. My bed is round, with a hole cut out to let my head through. Once

every hour a servant takes my temperature and gives me
another.

I have long subscribed to a fashion magazine. I wear a
white bonnet, white stockings, and a white waistcoat.

My doctor has always told me to smoke. Part of his advice
runs: "Smoke away, my dear chap. If you don't someone
else will."

Some musical performers become celebrated as much for
the crotchets in their behavior as for the ones they play.
One of the most widely admired pianists of the twentieth
century, Glenn Gould, is perhaps even more famous for his
eccentric performance habits and extreme hypochondria
than for his interpretive genius. He lived in deathly fear of
drafts, and habitually appeared on stage dressed for an arctic expedition—in the words of Leonard Bernstein, "doubly
hatted, doubly mittened, and endlessly muffled and muf-
flered."

In a conversation with a journalist, Gould once gave a
classic instance of the eccentric trait of the hypervivid imagination. When he was on tour in Israel in 1957, he was
having great interpretive difficulties with Beethoven's Piano
Concerto No. 2. He got into his rented car and drove out to
the middle of the desert near Tel Aviv. "I went out to a sand
dune, and decided that the only thing that could possibly
save this concert was to re-create the most admirable tactile
circumstances I knew of." They proved to be associated
with the old Chickering upright piano at his parents' summer cottage, which he had played as a boy. Gould re-
created the cottage in every detail in his mind, imagining
every piece of furniture, including the Chickering, and he

proceeded to "play" the entire concerto on the mental piano, without lifting a finger. "I got to the auditorium in the evening, played the concert, and it was without question the first time that I'd been in a really exalted mood throughout the entire stay there."

The annals of the eccentrics in the arts are vast enough to fill several volumes: Emily Dickinson always wore white, never went out of her room, and hid her poems in little boxes. James Joyce always carried with him a tiny pair of lady's bloomers, which he waved in the air to demonstrate approval. The American composer Charles Ives expended a great deal of time and money advocating an amendment to the U.S. Constitution that would limit the private income of all Americans to $20,000 a year. The eccentricities of Salvador Dalí have filled a number of books, though in his case there lingers the suspicion that it was perhaps as much show business as genuine eccentricity.

While attention naturally focuses on eccentrics who achieved great artistic success in their fields, there is a whole other breed of creative eccentric: those who are remarkably bad. Here are three spectacularly awful artists who had the courage and faith in themselves to persevere, despite the opprobrium heaped upon them.

Robert "Romeo" Coates (1772–1848), also called "The Celebrated Amateur of Fashion" and "Mr. Cockadoodle Coates," was execrated as England's worst actor in the Regency period. The son of a millionaire planter, he was born in Antigua, where he first performed Romeo, his signature role, in a version of the text that he himself had adapted. Once when he was corrected by a coach, Coates replied,

"Aye, that is the reading I know, for I have the whole play by heart, but I think I have improved on it." He always traveled with his Romeo costume, which was adorned with a fabulous collection of diamonds left him by his father.

Coates's unique style of acting was described by a reviewer in a fashionable periodical called *The Scourge:* "In the school of Coates, dignity is denoted by strutting across the stage in strides two yards long; agony by a furious stamp of the foot at the end of every second line." An actor in the Coates style "must learn to commit at least three mistakes in every line of the play," and "pronounce perfect 'purfet,' burden 'barden,' and memory 'memarry.' " He was easily baited, and several times in the course of his performance he would depart from the text to rebuke hecklers.

The highlight of Coates's Romeo was the death scene, which was always performed in exactly the same way: after his last line, he took his silk handkerchief, dusted off the stage, carefully laid down the handkerchief, placed his splendid plumed hat on top of it, and then died, depositing himself directly on top of his Juliet. On at least one occasion his death scene was received with such a terrific ovation that he sprang up, advanced to the edge of the stage and bowed to the audience, and then returned to his prostrate lover and died again. In 1814, when he played Romeo at Stratford, Coates visited the parish church and scribbled this graffito next to the bust of Shakespeare:

> His name in ambient air still floats
> And is adored by Robert Coates.
> Few loved ones have treated their adorer more harshly.

William "the Great" McGonagall has achieved immortality as the worst versifier the English language has yet produced. A weaver from Dundee, the Great McGonagall began his career as an actor in the Romeo Coates mold. In 1872 he bribed a theater manager in Edinburgh to let him play the title role in *Macbeth*. He was so entranced by the magical spell of the footlights that he refused to die at the play's end. Long after he had been run through by Macduff, he continued brandishing his sword and improvising bad verse. McGonagall was finally brought down when the actor playing Macduff lost his temper and gave him a good kick. The audience, of course, loved it: a star was born.

McGonagall earned his sobriquet "the Great" for his verse, which was unrelievedly dreary. He would take anything at all, however dull, as his subject, and render it in verse that was devoid of music and the basic elements of prosody. His first poem was about a local parson who had encouraged him:

> The first time I heard him speak
> 'Twas in the Kinnaird Hall,
> Lecturing on the Garibaldi Movement,
> As loud as he could bawl.

It continues in this vein, and ends with this couplet:

> May all good angels guard him while living,
> And hereafter, when he's dead.

The poet Hugh MacDiarmid, who devotes a chapter to McGonagall in *Scottish Eccentrics,* is probably right when he says that he "was not a bad poet; still less a good bad poet. He was not a poet at all." His editor, Lowden Macartney, described him as "a strange, weird, drab figure, who suggested more than anything else a broken-down actor. He wore his hair long and sheltered it with a wide-brimmed hat. His clothes were always shabby, and even in summer he refused to discard his overcoat. . . . He had a solemn, sallow face, with heavy features and eyes of the sort termed fish-like."

A true eccentric, he had a limitless belief in his own abilities, and was never discouraged by the relentless scorn of the world. Early in his career he addressed a poem to Queen Victoria, asking her to commission two of his masterpieces. Then, on the basis of a royal rejection slip he began styling himself "Poet to Her Majesty," and traveled by foot in a cold rain to Balmoral Castle to visit his coy patroness. To no avail; the queen was not amused, and was finally annoyed when McGonagall began insinuating in public that the appointment of Alfred, Lord Tennyson, to the post of poet laureate was a terrible mistake, and that he, McGonagall, should have been chosen.

No subject was too prosaic for McGonagall's muse. Here, for example, is his effusion on the opening of a new railway bridge in Dundee:

Beautiful new railway bridge of the silvery Tay,
With your strong brick piers and buttresses in so grand array,
And your thirteen central girders, which seem to my eye
Strong enough all windy storms to defy.
And as I gaze upon thee my heart feels gay,

Because thou art the greatest railway bridge of the present day,
And can be seen for miles away,
From north, south, east, or west of the Tay.

He supported himself by becoming a professional butt of
humor, a sort of poetical Oofty Goofty, hiring himself out to
student clubs where he would recite his wretched verse to
a roomful of drunken undergraduates, who pelted him with
verbal abuse and rotten vegetables. Despite the universal
scorn that greeted his work, he persevered in the belief that
he was the greatest poet in English since Shakespeare—a
conviction he proclaimed on many occasions in print.

What William McGonagall was to poetry, soprano Florence Foster Jenkins (1868–1944) was to singing. A wealthy
New York socialite from Wilkes-Barre, Pennsylvania, she
had a vivid image of herself as a diva, a goddess of song, but
no talent whatsoever. Her voice was quavery and colorless,
she was incapable of following a beat, and she sang wildly
out of tune; but she did have a vision, and the money and
courage to pursue it. Every year she gave a private recital at
the Ritz-Carlton Hotel. Accompanied by her pianist Cosme
McMoon, Jenkins gave inept performances of standard
opera arias and songs McMoon had written for her, such as
"Serenata Mexicano," filled with high coloratura passages
for her to mangle. Once word got around, tickets for the
spectacle were harder to come by than a box at the Met on
a Caruso night.

She made lavish costumes for her recitals, never fewer
than three per performance, which usually included the
Angel of Inspiration, a confection of silk, tinsel, and tulle,

with full feathered wings. After a taxicab accident in 1943, Jenkins reported that she could sing "a higher F than ever before"—thereby revealing her elastic concept of musical intonation. Rather than suing the taxicab company, she sent a box of cigars to the driver. Her final appearance was her Carnegie Hall debut, at the age of seventy-six; it was sold out weeks in advance. A month after this apotheosis, she died. Jenkins wrote her own epitaph: "Some people say I cannot sing, but no one can say I didn't sing."

FOUR

The scientists

Few people are capable of expressing with equanimity opinions which differ from the prejudices of their social environment. Most people are even incapable of forming such opinions.

—*Albert Einstein*

YVONNE X, CREATOR OF BERSERK PERPETUAL-MOTION MACHINES, WAS one of many exponents of eccentric science we encountered in the study. Eccentric science is that branch of learning, taught in no university curriculum, which rejects the imperative for reproducible results, favoring instead the impressionistic approach: it propounds what *ought* to be right. Whereas eccentric artists create their own strange worlds in their art, eccentric scientists use the world itself as their canvas, reinventing the physical universe to satisfy their creative impulses.

Almost exactly the same description might be applied to

the intellectual accomplishments of the great scientists of history, whose breakthrough theories form the basis of the orthodox science that *is* taught at universities. Many scientific giants were regarded as charlatans—or, worse, heretics—when they first articulated their revolutionary ideas; Galileo, Kepler, Harvey, Darwin, and Mendel are only a few of the most famous among them.

The fine line between genius and madness, proverbial even in ancient times, still exists in the sciences. If anything, it becomes finer the more we know about the universe and the more we learn about the human mind. Scientists themselves are increasingly uncertain about the difference between good science and bad science: overnight, the undisputed truth can become a discarded dead end, and its proponent the laughingstock of his profession, while the quirky little insight of a moment can disclose a whole new continent of thought. Both possibilities are exemplified in the career of Sir Isaac Newton. On the one hand, he devoted more of his time to studying alchemy than to what would nowadays be considered legitimate science, while on the other hand he could have had absolutely no idea when he invented differential calculus that he was setting off reverberations in the world economy that would last for three hundred years.

The drive for the masterstroke, one defining characteristic of genius, is often accompanied by a profound stubborn streak, an intractable resistance in the face of overwhelming opposition, which is similar to some traits and symptoms of obsession. But the eccentric scientist's steadfast faith in the rightness of his ideas in the face of derision may not be essentially different from the attitudes exhibited by conventional scientists.

Establishment science spontaneously rewrites its own history at every opportunity, enshrining what was once considered to be deviant, and smashing sacred icons with gleeful abandon once they have been discredited. Normal science tends to reject anything that is vague or indeterminate, for it has strict guidelines as to what qualifies as truth and a mania for maintaining a constant appearance of objectivity and validity. Eccentric scientists make no such pretense, and as a result they are afraid of nothing.

They are loners, and therefore less affected by social pressures to conform. If they have not already been ostracized by their colleagues, the prospect of ostracism does not daunt them in the least. But if our theories about the world are, as Karl Popper put it, at least in part "free creations of our own minds, the result of an almost poetic intuition," then scientists must have the freedom and the courage to take risks.

If the past is any guide, erroneous ways of searching ought to be encouraged or at least tolerated. At an empirical level, while some of the early Fellows of the Royal Society in London were making scientific discoveries that are still a part of basic science, others were doing work that was utterly without theory or purpose, and which indeed makes Yvonne X seem like a puristic exponent of the scientific method. Take, for instance, this excerpt from the society's experimental notes, dated July 24, 1616: "A circle was made with a powder of unicorn's horn, and a spider set in the middle of it, but it immediately ran out several times repeated. The spider once made some stay upon the powder."

As we have said, Newton spent a great deal of his time absorbed in alchemy; his laboratory assistant, Humphrey Newton (apparently no relation), reported that the great man stayed up all night long, poring over mystical texts, trying to change base metals into gold—hardly the paragon of sobersided rationalism portrayed by the modern university curriculum. Newton repeatedly said that the mathematical formulae in his *Principia* were universal truths revealed by God to a select group of mystical philosophers at the dawn of civilization, an esoteric tradition to which he considered himself heir—yet another aspect of his thought that modern scientists have conveniently allowed to slip into obscurity.

The history of science abounds with examples of errors that have fueled truth. For example, in 1844 the Scottish publisher Robert Chambers anonymously wrote a book entitled *Vestiges of the Natural History of Creation*. It postulated a law of constant progress and development, applying this premise to geology and the plant and animal worlds as well as the human species. In this last field, Chambers drew on phrenology, the notion that a person's mental characteristics could be discerned from the bumps and contours of his skull. Like Mary Wollstonecraft Shelley in *Frankenstein,* Chambers also believed that galvanic electricity had life-creating powers. Yet despite its many faulty premises, the *Vestiges* spurred Alfred Russel Wallace to undertake a series of expeditions to seek evidence for evolution, which in turn served as one of the principal inspirations to Darwin when he formulated his comprehensive theory on the subject. Although Wallace now occupies a more honorable place in the annals of science than does Robert Chambers, he, too, had his foibles; he was an enthusiastic follower of mesmerism, phrenology, and their hybrid offshoot, phrenomesmerism. Later, like many Victorian intellectuals, he was persuaded to embrace spiritualist beliefs and practices.

The hostility between institutional science and pseudoscience is a fairly recent phenomenon, and there are still some relics of their prior rapprochement: witness, for example, Sir Fred Hoyle's heterodox beliefs about microbial extraterrestrial life coming to this planet. The philosopher Paul Feyerabend has supported the argument that no single approach to the pursuit of knowledge should be allowed to dominate all others. Rival, even incompatible, theoretical approaches should be encouraged; as for methodology, anything goes, or should. Feyerabend encourages the toleration of eccentric science, and full, unhindered discourse between conventional and unconventional scientists. Eccentric scientists are often aggrieved at the way a hurried rejection of their ideas by a few establishment scientists can quickly produce a consensus in which the deviant ideas are rejected as foolish and irrational by people with no firsthand knowledge of them.

The history of science has repeatedly shown that it is the data which do not fit, the exceptions to the rule, that signal potential breakthroughs about the nature of the world. The search for misfit data can thus be considered as one among many legitimate approaches to science, alongside the experimental method and other conventional means. Eccentric science sometimes shows more variation than does orthodox science, and it can generate ideas and facts that may turn out, sooner or later, to be useful.

An excellent example of the value of eccentric science is provided by a group called the International Society of Cryptozoology, which is dedicated to searching for animal species not recognized by conventional science. Members of the group have organized expeditions into the wilderness of Northern California in search of Bigfoot, and to Scotland in pursuit of the Loch Ness monster. Roy Mackal, a biochemist at the University of Chicago and the society's vice president, is a believer in the existence of Mokele-mbembe, a huge beast that, legend holds, lurks in the swamps of the Congo jungle. Mackal contends that it may be a relict sauropod, a semiaquatic dinosaur of the Cretaceous period. In 1987 he published *A Living Dinosaur?,* an account of his expedition to the Congo in search of Mokele-mbembe. He found no monster, but he did hear a lot of stories from the local people; the book is filled with unintentionally ridiculous photographs, such as a picture of an empty pond with the caption, "Monsterpool where a Mokele-mbembe had been for several weeks." Another photograph, showing an empty patch of jungle, is captioned, "Path through underbrush made by Mokele-mbembe getting to the river."

Although cryptozoologists spend a great deal of time pursuing chimeras, they have also made a number of important contributions to "real" zoology. Richard Greenwell, the society's secretary, points out that of the 4,629 known mammal species, 1,827 were discovered this century. Most of them were found early in the century, when Africa and South America were first studied scientifically, but new animals are still being discovered. In 1991 James Mead, curator of marine mammals at the Smithsonian Institution and a member of the International Society of Cryptozoology, discovered the Peruvian beaked whale. In 1975 the first specimen of the Chacoan peccary, previously known only from fossils, was found in Paraguay. In Vietnam an entirely new genus, *Pseudoryx,* was discovered in 1993 by zoologist John MacKinnon.

Eccentric scientists are fascinated by everything, and they often make connections that orthodox science would consider to be beyond the pale. They love data that coincide unexpectedly, and typically take the mere existence of a coincidence as proof of their thesis. A practicing alchemist in our study discovered several ancient hieroglyphics in the shape of a double helix. This led him to ask if the ancients had knowledge of recombinant DNA. Another eccentric scientist in the study, Henry Alelove, found a similar cosmic connection while perfecting a new invention. In his own words:

> For years I have agonized over phenomena which were aberrations. Allow me to explain. After patenting my orbital engine, I became interested in the possibility of shifting a ten-ton, cement-hulled boat over rough ground by man-

power and ingenuity. I developed a set of walking feet and horizontal jacks which were secured to the boat, and by turning a cam the boat progressed slowly to the water. It would have worked, but the owner of the boat came into some money and the need evaporated.

By this time, I was expert in turning my novel circular cams. It stimulated me to ask, "How fast must the cams be turned before the boat would no longer have time to follow the cam and would in fact be hovering?" I took a guess from a creature in nature that can hover, namely the blowfly. I found its pitch to be about 64 hertz. I recorded this sound as I released a fly trapped in a cobweb. When I played the tape back, at the point where the fly became airborne, and nowhere else, pellets of shot in a horizontal speaker lifted off the cone, as did talcum powder on a paper sheet placed across the speaker. I concluded that, at 64 hertz, mass detaches itself from the force of gravity. Now 64 hertz is very near C two octaves below middle C. It is the same sound that the Buddhist monk makes when he chants his *om mane padme hum*. It is the sound of a bee on a drowsy summer's day.

At this point orthodox science screamed with laughter. I was referred to a series of science "nuts"—characters who talk of sine waves and resonance, and then bird-watchers and porpoise fanciers. Incidentally, the "nuts" are very close to the truth, however narrow were their fields. I have been put on the Establishment's "Don't read, just dump" list. I have not decided what to call this work, but a colleague has trimmed it down to "The Philosophy of Tetrahedronalism and Its Tetradental Metaphysics and Metamathematics." After reading it you will be ready to "Do the right thing." You have been warned.

It was the very improbability of a congruence existing between such vastly disparate elements that gave the discovery its significance to the eccentric scientist: to him, any coincidence so striking must be true. Yet that line of reasoning—that ideas or symbols found recurring in completely unrelated areas must somehow form a meaningful connection—is almost universal, as is the intuitive feeling that such a finding must be true, precisely because of its improbability. A rumor may have no truth to it whatsoever; but we are far more likely to believe even the most preposterous tale if we hear it from two independent sources. For the eccentric, that sort of coincidence is the only confirmation necessary.

For that reason, eccentrics' science is strongly theory-led, rather than data-based. Their theories result from an ongoing process in which no assumptions or ideas are out of bounds, and as a result they often fail to adhere to the criteria that govern orthodox experimental science. For example, a theory that succeeds is usually validated by its predictive power. To that end, the theorist formulates alternative working hypotheses and anticipates other conceptual frameworks that might more reasonably account for the observations. A successful theory should possess a reasonable degree of reliability, and be able to be reproduced in similar, or sometimes slightly different, circumstances.

Deviant theories—for example, those concerning perpetual-motion machines, extrasensory perception, psychokinesis, Erich von Däniken's claims that extraterrestrial aliens have influenced human history, and Immanuel Velikovsky's ideas about planetary catastrophes—do not fulfill the above minimum criteria. However, some widely accepted theories also fail to meet these standards. Many of the basic tenets of Freudian psychoanalysis and cultural anthropology, for instance, have at best only partial credibility when evaluated by these rigid standards.

The staying power of these two fields is a proof of the adage that nothing succeeds like success. The dramatic, seemingly miraculous cures brought about by Freud and his early colleagues helped to establish psychoanalysis as vastly superior to previous theories about the mind. Likewise, the theories of Franz Boas and Ruth Benedict were pioneering first attempts to examine world cultures systematically, and represented a great advance over the biased and haphazard reports of their predecessors. Yet a century on, both these fields are beginning to show their age, and the original theories they are based upon might be regarded as deviant science that got lucky—much as early heliocentrists such as Tycho Brahe and even Galileo, while they were right in the essentials, muddled over and through some very important issues.

The most important point at which conventional and eccentric scientists part company is at the phase of post-inspiration critical analysis. The conventional scientist is consumed with doubts, and is constantly scripting scenarios in which his theory turns out to be mistaken or artifactual. He feels compelled to check his data over and over again, working into the small hours, seven days a week. One highly respected scientist acquired the nickname "El Flagello" because of the lengths to which he took his soul-searching.

But for the eccentric scientist, concerns about validation

or confirmation are ignored in the intoxicating rush that accompanies discovery. Once the breakthrough has been made, the scientist typically feels himself to be propelled forward to make future conquests. His talent for imaginative elaboration seems to him to be limitless. While it is usually a liability for a scientist not to treat his findings from a critical perspective, eccentrics have as a compensation the indefatigable optimism of their breed. They are frequently dynamic advocates for their ideas. Witness this brief summary of one eccentric inventor's travails:

> In the recent past I have been short-listed for a post writing sales brochures for airships, divested myself of a small fortune building and subsequently dismantling a boat in my dining-room, conducted a lengthy correspondence with professors at two universities about prone-piloted aircraft, and had a draft patent description on surface-skimming vehicles withdrawn by the Patent Office for review by the Inventions Unit of the Ministry of Defence. Daunted, I submitted one last design for a signature verification system, but went into computer management instead. I have some interesting applications for liquid crystal arrays, though the time and inclination are not as easy to find nowadays.

Eccentric scientists often have their best ideas rejected. To rationalize these setbacks, they sometimes develop unrelated theories to accommodate the continuous misunderstandings they encounter. Here is one typical account:

> When I set out to produce some inventions, I deliberately chose to cover a broad range. I have never had a proposal

receive serious consideration from a manufacturer, even my Stock Exchange game. I have written literally dozens of letters about my Innovation Centre idea to various government departments involved in unemployment and education, etc., to politicians who have had a lot to say about unemployment, to various notable people who ought to have been interested, and the response has varied between indifference and lukewarm negative interest. The professionally involved are often guilty of arrogant negligence. I believe inventors fall into the trap of the perpetual-motion machine through the sheer frustration of having perfectly reasonable commercial ideas ignored. I came to the conclusion that antagonism to innovators is so consistent as to indicate some deep-rooted psychological basis. Hence my interest in the work showing that dominant male vervet monkeys behave in a typical fashion, and have an invariable increase in serotonin levels. My theory is that submissive signals are even more subtle than is generally recognized, and that innovators or eccentrics do not conform to the usual pattern for some reason, which may be an obscure combination of many factors.

As strange as this monkey-gland theory of eccentricity might seem, if we have learned just one lesson from deviant science, it is that we should not dismiss any idea out of hand, no matter how implausible it might seem: good science has been spun from stranger stuff than that.

One of the classic instances of an eccentric scientist having his ideas at first ridiculed and then ultimately vindicated is James Burnett, Lord Monboddo (1714–99). Lord Monboddo was a Scottish jurist and amateur natural historian and linguist who published a learned, six-volume treatise called *The Origin and Progress of Language,* the first scientific work to suggest that man is descended from the apes. He claimed that the human tailbone is a vestige of our simian ancestry—a detail he may have regretted mentioning, for he was the butt of tail jokes for the rest of his life. Boswell reports that when he and Dr. Johnson visited Lord Monboddo in 1773, "Sir Adolphus Oughton laughed at Lord Monboddo's notion of men having tails and called him a Judge *a posteriori* which amused Dr. Johnson." Johnson's own verdict on Monboddo concluded with one of his most famous witticisms:

> It is a pity to see Lord Monboddo publish such notions as he has done: a man of sense, and of so much elegant learning. There would be little in a fool doing it; we should only laugh; but when a wise man does it we are sorry. Other people have strange notions; but they conceal them. If they have tails they hide them; but Monboddo is as jealous of his tail as a squirrel.

In the light of Darwin's theory of evolution some seventy years later, we are not inclined to find the notion of man and the apes being linked in their remote ancestry to be quite as laughable as did his lordship's contemporaries. Despite his disdain for Monboddo's theories, by the end of his visit to him at his estate in Kincardineshire Johnson had found in the old Scotsman a kindred spirit—further proof, if any were needed, that the Great Cham of Literature was himself an eccentric. Nonetheless, he loved to poke fun at

Monboddo. He laughed at his host's calling himself Farmer Burnett and going about wearing a little round hat. Monboddo, in true eccentric style, called himself an enthusiastical farmer, which Johnson found ridiculous: "For (said he) what can he do in farming by his *enthusiasm*?" That is uncharacteristically dogmatic for Johnson: would his dictionary ever have been completed if he had not been an enthusiastical lexicographer?

Lord Monboddo never rode in a carriage, even in advanced old age, for he believed it was an affront to human dignity to ride behind a horse rather than mounted on top of it. In 1785, after one of his rides from Edinburgh to London, he visited the King's Bench. There was an accident and some of the hall's fixtures gave way, causing the lawyers and judges to scatter and run for the exits. Then, according to Hugh MacDiarmid, "Monboddo, somewhat near-sighted and rather dull of hearing, sat still, and was the only man who did so. Being asked why he had not bestirred himself to avoid the ruin, he coolly answered that he 'thought it was an annual ceremony with which, being an alien, he had nothing to do' "—a classic instance of eccentric reasoning.

While Monboddo's theories had to wait until more than fifty years after his death to be vindicated (at least in part), many of the ideas produced by eccentric science achieve immediate success. In fact, most of the inventors in the study succeeded in receiving patents. Among their inventions are the seemingly bizarre and frivolous—a magnetized shower curtain, an electric ruler, a water-powered toothbrush—as well as genuinely important contributions to science. One subject developed a powerful new antibiotic, another a cheap and effective solar power system. The superefficient square exhaust pipes now to be seen on the rear of the Concorde were developed by an eccentric inventor in the study. One of our subjects was the first man in Britain to carry a child in a backpack in public, which got his picture on the front page of *The Times;* another claims, plausibly, that he was the first person to listen to the radio on headphones in the street. Some of the inventors, such as our junkist, John Ward, make machines that are useless but are delightful creations to behold. Another designs marvelous, fanciful, high-performance kites.

Often, eccentric scientists are motivated by the selfless humanitarianism typical of their kind. One inventor in the study proposed a number of elaborate methods for cleaning up oil spills in the ocean. In one plan, the oil slick is first broken up into smaller particles by chemical means. Overflying aircraft would then drop millions of tiny iron slivers, individually encased in polypropylene to keep them afloat. The oil would stick to the floaters, he theorized, which would then be attracted to magnetic plates in long cylinders slung over the bows of six naval auxiliary vessels. An alternative to the magnetic technique would use powerful electric pumps fitted with bellows mechanisms to provide a suction force. There are several difficulties with these plans; according to expert marine engineers we consulted, the biggest problem is that the formidable volume of oil usually lost in such spills would overwhelm these systems, even if they performed at peak efficiency.

The proposals of some eccentric scientists and inventors

might have worked, except that they were simply too grandiose to be implemented. One developed a system that took as its mission nothing less than to avert the next Ice Age, whenever it threatens. He proposed warming deep-sea water by heat induction and transfer. Heat-trap buoys would support massive aluminum pipes, reaching nearly two miles below the surface, in a belt 1,600 miles wide along the equator. Sunlight would heat the pipes at the top. When the tops were warmer than the nearby sea water, the water inside would begin to rise, and more cold water would flow into the bottom openings.

This inventor also believed that it would be possible to increase the total sunshine on earth by 1 percent or more, by placing a belt of spherical mirror satellites in orbit. The goal for this system was to melt the snow and ice boundaries back to their 1940 summer limits. Sir Fred Hoyle warned that such projects might cause a dangerous rise in sea levels, but our inventor parried that objection with an equally modest proposal for the mass construction of sea walls to protect all the world's ports.

In the days before academic specialization, scientists were much more indulgent of the penchant for eccentricity in their personal lives than they are nowadays. Some of the greatest scientists and inventors of the past gave free rein to peculiar habits that, if they were alive today, they might need to conceal:

- Benjamin Franklin took "air baths" for his health, by sitting naked in front of an open window and breathing deeply. Lord Monboddo also practiced nudism, as did

Charles Richter, the inventor of the earthquake scale named after him.

- Alexander Graham Bell covered the windows of his house to keep out the pernicious rays of the full moon. He also tried to teach his dog how to talk.

- The evolutionary philosopher Herbert Spencer, who coined the phrase "survival of the fittest," wore velvet earplugs and a bulky one-piece garment of his own design when he was home, as an aid to concentration. His friends said behind his back that he resembled a deaf bear.

Henry Cavendish (1731–1810) was among the most brilliant scientists in history. He was the first person to realize that water was not a single element but rather was composed of hydrogen and oxygen. He also measured the density of the earth and discovered (but neglected to publish) two fundamental principles of electricity—Coulomb's Law and Ohm's Law—years before Charles Coulomb and Georg Ohm thought of them. Cavendish was shy and introverted to a highly eccentric degree. He never received guests, and ordered his dinner daily by leaving a note for the cook on the hall table. To ensure that he would never have to have personal contact with his servants, he developed an elaborate system of double doors within his house. Once he met a maid on the staircase by accident, and the experience so upset him that he had a second stairway built to spare himself any more such encounters. At a certain point Cavendish's selective avoidance of people probably amounted to a social phobia.

His contemporary Lord Brougham recalled Cavendish's nervous quirks at scientific meetings—"the shrill cry he uttered as he shuffled quickly from room to room, seeming to be annoyed if looked at. . . . He probably uttered fewer words in the course of his life than any man who ever lived to fourscore years, not at all excepting the monks of La Trappe." Like those of many eccentrics, Cavendish's interests were catholic and wide-ranging; he published a paper in the *Notes* of the Royal Society about the Hindu calendar.

The first recorded eccentric in Los Angeles, a place that later came to be known as a world-class center of weirdness, devoted most of his life to science. William Money was a poor Scots lad, born with what looked like a rainbow in his right eye, who worked his passage across the Atlantic. He soon made his way to Mexico, where he was issued a passport as a naturalist by the president. He trekked by himself through the Sonoran desert into unexplored regions of northern Mexico, drawing hundreds of maps of the area and collecting a vast number of botanical and zoological specimens. Over the course of twenty years, he wrote some 30,000 pages of notes.

By 1846, now a self-taught doctor, Money was married to a beautiful local girl and had become a leading citizen of the little town of Los Angeles, then still in Mexico. War with the United States was brewing, and Money decided to flee. He packed up all his possessions and headed south. One night his camp was ambushed, first by American troopers and then by Indians, and in the ensuing scuffle Money's lifework, all of his specimens and notes, was destroyed, blown away by the desert winds.

The loss cracked him. He spent the next sixteen years pressing a quixotic claim for a quarter of a million dollars against the U.S. government, but only succeeded in losing his money and his family. What little money he managed to hold on to he sank into a hacienda near San Gabriel, California, a brick and adobe fantasia based on his childhood memories of Holyrood Palace in Edinburgh, complete with turrets, towers, buttresses, and bastions. He established a new religion, a fundamentalist sect called the Reformed New Testament Church of the Faith of Jesus Christ, with himself as bishop and spiritual leader.

In later life Money dedicated himself to eccentric science in its purest form. He drew a global map that showed a subterranean ocean extending from the North Pole to the South Pole. A hole in the Arctic ice cap sucked water from the known seas into the subterranean ocean, where it was heated by volcanic activity. The heated water rushed out at the Antarctic in two-mile-wide streams, which he called the Kuro Siwa. As fanciful as his science was, like Lord Monboddo, Money got some things right: he correctly observed that the earth's crust in the San Francisco Bay area was very thin, and in 1872 predicted that an earthquake would destroy the city—thirty-four years before the great quake of 1906.

A lady from Pasadena visited Money at the end of his life, and published this eyewitness account in a local newspaper:

Quaintest of all the objects which arrested the eye of the visitor at Mission San Gabriel were the pretentious gateway and beehive piers of the Moneyan Institute. These led to a more ambitious structure in the rear in which a school was kept by the founder. Upon the double gate inscriptions in Greek, Latin, and Hebrew bore witness to the value of learning. Even the cuneiform characters of ancient Nineveh were inwrought as decoration. . . . In one of the remaining piers the old fanatic died, with an image of the Holy Virgin above his head, an articulated skeleton at his feet, and a well-worn copy of some Greek classic within reach of his hand.

Today medicine is closely associated with chemistry, but in the past there were healers who looked to physics for the causes of illness, and for cures. Franz Anton Mesmer (1734–1815) thought he found a link between health and magnetism, and like other eccentric scientists, once he had found the connection, he devoted a lifetime to proselytizing his great discovery. Having first prepared for the priesthood and then for the law in his native Austria, he obtained his medical qualifications at the rather late age of thirty-three.

Mesmer brought current theories of astronomy and Newton's law of gravitation into his biological model of animal magnetism. His theory assumed that there was an ethereal fluid present in all living things, similar to the *chi* of Chinese medicine, which was responsible for the organism's vitality. Good health, he concluded, results when this inner magnetic fluid is in balance with the magnetic fluid that fills the universe. If the equilibrium got out of whack, order could be restored by pulling the fluids back into alignment with magnets.

At first Mesmer simply fitted small magnets onto various

parts of his patients' bodies. He moved to Paris, where he had a spectacular success; he once refused 20,000 livres for his secret. Soon he progressed to group healing at his lavishly appointed clinic, where patients sat around a tub filled with water and iron powder, and held tight to iron bars protruding from its sides.

Mesmer was widely criticized by the medical establishment, and he didn't help his case by the increasing theatricality of his performances. Before long, the group treatments resembled séances. Mesmer's powerful, charismatic personality assumed a more important part in the ceremonies, which he presided over wearing a lilac cloak and waving an iron wand. He finally abandoned the use of magnets and began channeling the cosmic fluid through his own body and, via the iron wand, into his patients.

While Mesmer's theory of animal magnetism was, of course, without any foundation in fact, he did make a lasting contribution to science with the invention of hypnotism, which used to be known as mesmerism. This is an excellent example of eccentric serendipity (a word coined by Horace Walpole, who was an eccentric): while Mesmer's iron wand and theory of animal magnetism are now synonymous with bunkum, his hypnotic technique is still in use today in legitimate medicine, with a multitude of practical applications.

FIVE

Lost Continents and Golden Ages

The broadest and most prevalent error requires the most disinterested virtue to sustain it.

—*Henry David Thoreau,* Walden

MESMER STANDS AT A PECULIARLY ECCENTRIC CONFLUENCE, WHERE science, mysticism, and religion meet. Many meandering streams have their sources there. Some of the traits most frequently associated with eccentrics—optimistic idealism, originality, heightened imagination, indifference to the approval of society—can produce a bitter disappointment with life as it is and motivate the eccentric to dream dreams that have all the vividness of reality.

Many of the eccentric scientists in the study straddle the line between religion and science, sometimes displaying considerable intellectual freedom in the way they appropriate bits and pieces of many different disciplines to support their ideas. Often they openly acknowledge the heterodoxy of their approach. One middle-aged woman, an astrophysicist whose projects include an attempt to prove the existence of leprechauns using satellite surveillance, told us, "I grab bits out of the Bible and put my own interpretations on them. One of them is, 'The lily of the field neither slumbers nor sleeps.' I equate 'field' with the electromagnetic field, humming away merrily, telling us things day in and day out. With a considerable amount of training for mental hygiene, one is able to filter the incoming information for what are good and what are bad signposts."

Another eccentric scientist told us that his theories came to him by a visionary process, "as brain-waves from a spiritual reservoir." From his study of physics, he composed "a mathematical-metaphysical-UFO theory—the first and only one as far as I know—together with a creation theory, according to which the expanding universe is not contrary to Newton's law of gravitation. I announced my theory of the descent of man in an extensive syllabus called 'Our Metaphysical-Biblical World Picture.' Science is nothing else but devising theories out of a field of knowledge, and that knowledge is an important theme in the Bible. I became scientifically converted to Christianity."

Such a creative, visionary approach has an impressive pedigree, of course. The apocalyptic visions of Blake and the midnight alchemy of Newton are both expressions of dissatisfaction with the limitations of reality and attempts to reinvent the world radically. Yet for all the prophetic fervor of Blake's visions, they are poetry, and do not pretend to a higher state of reality than that of art. Newton and other alchemists, despite the magic encrusted on their work, were trying to transmute the base metals of the real world into real gold.

There are, however, eccentric visions that go further and postulate that if the world we see around us is limited and disappointing, then we must find the brave and better new world that exists beyond the one we can see and touch. This place may take the form, through myth, of a golden age that existed here on earth in the past, or to take it a step higher, may exist in the realm of metaphysics, in the beyond.

Here, admittedly, we are veering into treacherous waters, for these are matters not of opinion but of belief. Myth is what we call someone else's religion; our own we call revelation. The gnomic mysticism of Jesus, for example, if it were possible to view his teachings objectively, might be seen as eccentric—or it might not. Yet it is very difficult to view dispassionately the life of anyone as influential as Jesus. Likewise, his philosophy, as recorded in the Gospels, is so profound a part of world civilization that it is equally difficult to consider it apart from the historical fact that throughout the past two thousand years a great part of humanity has viewed his mystical utterances as a revelation of transcendental truth. Exactly the same sentences might be written about Gautama Buddha or Mohammed. The messages of these men were galvanized by their personal charisma, which may have arisen in part from their extreme goodness.

Yet we might not feel it necessary to be quite so scrupulous about Joseph Smith, the American prophet who claimed that on September 22, 1827, when he was fourteen years old, an angel named Moroni appeared to him and told him where he might dig up golden tablets inscribed with a lengthy divine revelation. The tablets were written in a strange hieroglyphic system called Reformed Egyptian, but Moroni supplied young Smith with two stones, the mysterious Urim and Thummim of the Old Testament, which transformed the writing into English. The tablets, purportedly the work of an ancient prophet called Mormon, were a fanciful history of America during biblical times. After the confusion of tongues at the Tower of Babel, a man named Jared sailed across the Atlantic and founded a prosperous civilization in America. It ended in a terrible civil war in upstate New York, in which everyone except one man died. Then a man from Jerusalem named Lehi, in the time of Zedekiah, emigrated to America with his family. They met the last Jaredite but did not profit by his example, for there was another civil war, at the same spot in New York. The survivors of this calamity became the American Indians.

Smith published this yarn as *The Book of Mormon* and founded the Church of Latter-Day Saints based upon its wisdom. Much of what was written on Moroni's golden tablets bears a strong resemblance to a romance published twenty-five years earlier by an American parson named Solomon Spaulding; moreover, it would seem to be damning that no archaeological evidence of the Jaredite occupation of America has yet been excavated. Nonetheless, millions of devout Mormons believe that Smith's visions were genuine, and they would consider the suggestion that he was a fraud to be offensive and even blasphemous.

It is far more likely that Joseph Smith was an eccentric

with a humanitarian vision than an outright fraud, for his life after Moroni's appearance strongly supports the sincerity of his beliefs. It is possible that Spaulding's story sank into Smith's subconscious when he read it and then reappeared later, at a moment of personal crisis, as a dream or hallucination, complete with a framework for lucid interpretation. (In a similar vein, psychologists believe that people who recall previous lives while under hypnosis are drawing upon a well-stocked memory derived from prior reading or viewing.) Yet devout Mormons would hardly be more persuaded, or less offended, by a determination of benign eccentricity than by an accusation of fraud, no matter how overwhelming the proof might be.

A religious cultist who was certainly eccentric was Elspeth Buchan (1738–91), a Scottish woman who proclaimed herself as the personal vehicle of salvation. She identified herself with the first verse of Revelation, Chapter 12: "There appeared a great wonder in Heaven; a woman clothed with the sun, and the moon under her feet, and upon her head a crown of twelve stars." She was abetted by the Reverend Hugh Whyte, a minister of the Relief Church (later to become a part of the United Presbyterian Church) who was her chief apostle. Whyte preached that God Himself would soon appear to Buchan, who was known as "Friend Mother in the Lord," and her followers, and translate them directly to Heaven, without anyone having the bother of dying first. More controversially, Whyte claimed that divine vengeance and the flames of Hell would be visited upon all those Scotsmen who refused to acknowledge Mother Buchan as God's personal emissary. That kind of talk was more than the good people of Tayside could bear, and so they periodically rose up and rioted against the Buchanites, who moved from town to town like gypsies, much as the Mormons in America were later to do.

Mother Buchan's interpretations of the Bible were quite literal, and her belief in divine guidance absolute. Once, when the sect was running low on funds, she announced that she had had a revelation that Heaven was about to supply them with money. She directed a member of the congregation to join her in the street, where they stood holding a sheet, waiting for cash to fall from the sky. After a while the man got tired and left Mother Buchan to stand there alone. A short while later, she appeared holding a five-pound note, saying that the man's lack of faith was the reason the stipend was so stingy and slow in coming.

One day the Rev. Whyte announced that the moment of the cult's triumphant translation to Heaven was imminent, and Mother Buchan ordered the faithful to fast for forty days, to lighten the load. The historian A. S. Morton describes the ensuing debacle:

> The fateful night at length arrived, and the expectant company assembled on rising ground near the house, where they sang and prayed till midnight. They then proceeded to Templand Hill, the appointed scene of translation, half a mile away. Here they erected a frail wooden staging, which they mounted, with Mother Buchan on a higher platform in the middle. They had all cut their hair short (except Mother Buchan), leaving only a tuft on the top, by which they could be caught up from above, and on their feet they had light

bauchels [Scots: old shoes] which they could easily kick off when the moment came to ascend. The air was filled with their singing and invocations as they stood stretching their hands to the rising sun. Suddenly a gust of wind swept along, the flimsy platform collapsed, and instead of ascending to Heaven they crashed down to earth.

One of the basic tenets of Mother Buchan's creed was that she herself could not die. When she fell sick and it became increasingly clear that the prophecy of her immortality was about to be confounded, she announced to her followers that she might *appear* to die, but in fact she was going to heaven to prepare the way for them. She promised to return in six months to escort them to paradise. If their faith was not sufficient, then she would give them a second chance and return again in ten years. If that failed, she would come back in fifty years to announce the end of the world.

A few days later she died. The six-month and ten-year anniversaries came and went uneventfully; by the time of the fiftieth anniversary, only two Buchanites were left, a man named Andrew Innes and his wife. After the day ended without an appearance by Mother Buchan, Innes confessed to his friends that he still had the prophetess's body in his possession. When he died, he directed that she be buried with him—but her coffin must be placed under his own, he said, so that she would not be able to ascend to Heaven without bringing him along.

Given that we have no way of determining whether someone's revelation is genuine—for that would assume

From 1859 until his death in 1880 Joshua Abraham Norton was the self-proclaimed emperor of the United States. His popularity was such that when he died 30,000 of his "subjects" attended his funeral. *(New York Public Library)*

Ann Atkin shares her home and grounds in Devon with 7,500 garden gnomes. *(Derek Hudson/Sygma)*

Inventor John Ward describes himself as a "junkist" who likes "to put rubbish to good use," as in the creation of his Bod-Pod. (*Courtesy John Ward*)

"Humor is an integral part of healing," says Dr. Patch Adams, and he practices what he preaches. He holds a conventional medical degree, but is highly unconventional in that he accepts no payment of any kind for treating his patients. (*Josef Astor*)

Gary Holloway is an environmental planner, but the real center of his life is his varied eccentricities, notably the fan club he established in memory of Martin Van Buren, the eighth and least-appreciated U.S. president. He finds a Franciscan monk's habit both comfortable and convenient to wear. *(Josef Astor)*

The career of Victoria Claflin Woodhull, caricatured here by Thomas Nast, included glamour, scandal, and feminism; she was an advocate of free love, and was the first woman candidate for the U.S. presidency. *(New York Public Library)*

To Jack Mytton the spice of life was not variety but danger, and he could not understand why other people felt differently. When a friend said he had never been in a carriage accident, Mytton exclaimed, "What a damned slow fellow you must have been all your life!" and promptly overturned their gig. *(New York Public Library)*

Artists Peter McGough and David McDermott re-created the nineteenth century in their New York apartment and studio and wore only period clothes. *(Josef Astor)*

Collar turned up against real or imaginary drafts, pianist Glenn Gould hunches over the keyboard. *(Sony Classical)*

AN AMATEURS DREAM. "Is this that Gallant Gay Lothario." Published for the Satirist Ltd.

Robert Coates acquired his nickname of "Romeo" because he played that role so often and so badly, usually in his own "improved" version of the text. His death scene was particularly notorious.
(New York Public Library)

Her dress sense was as freakish as her singing: Soprano Florence Foster Jenkins is seen here attired in a confection entitled "The Angel of Inspiration."
(New York Public Library)

Probably the worst poet Britain has ever produced, William "the Great" McGonagall had no truck with rhythm, prosody, or syntax. Undaunted by Queen Victoria's refusal to commission poems from him and jealous of the poet laureate, Tennyson, he styled himself "Poet to Her Majesty."
(Dundee Art Galleries and Museums)

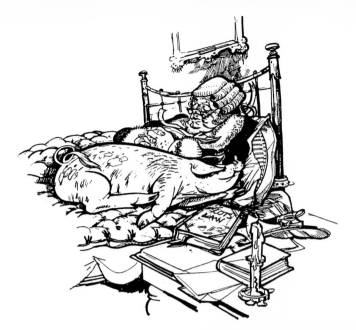

James Burnett, Lord
Monboddo, caricatured here
by Ian Bailey, is one of the
many eccentric scientists
whose ideas have later been
vindicated. His treatise *The
Origin and Progress of
Language,* published
seventy years before
Darwin's *On the Origin of
Species,* proposed that man
is descended from the apes.
*(Scottish National Portrait
Gallery)*

Most of Franz Mesmer's theories
have been discarded, but
hypnosis, originally known
as mesmerism, is still used
in medicine today.
(New York Public Library)

"The Ladies of Llangolen," the Rt. Hon. Eleanor Butler and Miss Sarah Ponsonby. They retreated from the world to live together in a secluded cottage in Wales.
(British Museum)

John Slater is the only person to have walked barefoot from Land's End to John O'Groats dressed in pajamas. He has made his home in a cave in the Western Highlands of Scotland, undeterred by the fact that it is flooded at high tide.
(Derek Hudson/Sygma)

Dot Griffiths, seen here with her husband, Reg, is able both to practice and to teach Wicca (white magic) without fear of persecution at her home near Milton Keynes, England.
(Derek Hudson/Sygma)

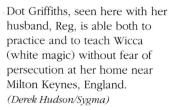

Lillie Hitchcock Coit's obsession with fire engines and fire-fighting began during her childhood in San Francisco. In her teens she was made an honorary member of the Knickerbocker Engine Company No. 5, and for the rest of her long life she always wore the company's gilded badge.
(New York Public Library)

that we could agree on basic metaphysical principles, something that occurs only fitfully even among people who belong to the same religion—we can try to look at such matters objectively. We may say, in the first place, that religion-founding was a much more common activity when Gautama Buddha, Jesus, and Mohammed were doing it. That is not to say that they had any inherent advantage over Joseph Smith or Mother Buchan, except for the gentle patina that a few thousand years endows, which tends to soften any factual irregularities. Modern biblical scholarship is largely devoted to the business of showing which earlier prophetic texts Jesus or the authors of the Gospels drew upon to create the body of Christian revelation—which is not materially different from pointing out that *The Book of Mormon* was based upon Solomon Spaulding's romance. Yet it is probably true that the very nature of consciousness and thought has changed since the time of Jesus or Buddha. Mysticism was in the air they breathed, just as it is said to be in India. But Scotland in the eighteenth century and upstate New York in the nineteenth century were not mystical places, and those who practiced religion-founding there are at least candidates for eccentricity.

More often, modern myths have taken on the forms of science, history, and geography, which are used to buttress arguments for the actual existence of a golden age. The classic instance of that sort of eccentric mythopoesis is the persistent belief in the lost continent of Atlantis. It is a particularly good example, for it requires a comparison between classical myth, where Atlantis makes its first appearance, and modern pseudoscience and pseudohistory, where it has continued to thrive—to say nothing of popular culture.

The earliest surviving references to the legendary continent of Atlantis are to be found in two dialogues by Plato, the *Timaeus* and the *Critias*. According to Plato, the Athenian lawgiver Solon traveled to Egypt, where the priests of the goddess Neith (whom Plato identified with Athena) told him that the Greeks' conception of history was only fragmentary, and that many civilizations had existed before the ones they knew about. The priests told Solon that nine thousand years earlier Athena herself had established a city at the site of Athens, which waged a war against a "great and wonderful empire" called Atlantis. Atlantis was an enormous island, bigger than Asia and Libya combined, outside the Pillars of Hercules (the Strait of Gibraltar) in the Atlantic Ocean.

Atlantis controlled most of the Mediterranean west of Greece and wanted to conquer the rest, but the ancient Athenians (ancient, that is, even to Solon, himself almost a legendary figure to Plato's readers) waged a terrible war against Atlantis. Against all odds, the Athenians prevailed, even after their allies had deserted the cause. Then a cataclysmic earthquake and flood destroyed Athens and its army, and caused the whole continent of Atlantis to sink beneath the ocean.

There is much more. In the *Critias,* Plato goes into great detail about the geography, history, and political system of Atlantis, though he never does get around to the promised chronicle of the Atheno-Atlantean war. The dialogue ends in midsentence—only the first of the mysteries connected with Atlantis. Not least among them is what Plato's intentions were in these dialogues. It is tempting to agree with Aristotle and take the myth of Atlantis as just that, a didactic fantasy meant, like the myths in the *Republic,* to illustrate the author's theories about the ideal state and correct human behavior. Nonetheless, the tone of Plato's Atlantis writings has nothing of the patently allegorical "once upon a time" about it; he writes very much as though it was a real place. Moreover, if it is an instructive parable, it is unclear exactly what the message is, which is singularly un-Platonic.

For these reasons there have always been people who have wanted to believe in the historicity of Atlantis. Sir Francis Bacon set a utopian romance there *(The New Atlantis),* and the Jesuit polymath Athanasius Kircher published a map of it in 1665. Of course, belief in the existence of Atlantis was not in itself eccentric. The works of Plato have always been widely read, and it was perfectly reasonable to believe in the great dialoguist's lost continent until modern geology and archaeology made it quite obvious, from a scientific point of view, that there could never have been a great continent in the Atlantic. Yet it was at just that point in time, in the middle of the nineteenth century, that the great Atlantean revival began.

The eccentric spirit asserted itself in determined attempts to prove what appeared, with increasing certainty, to be unprovable because untrue. What the perpetual-motion machine is to eccentric physics, the lost continent of Atlantis is to eccentric geography: if establishment geologists and archaeologists say it is impossible, that only proves how limited is their vision. In every field, the eccentric welcomes the impossible as a challenge.

The modern cult of Atlantis was in large measure created by a Minnesotan named Ignatius T. T. Donnelly. In 1882 he published a massive book called *Atlantis: The Antediluvian World,* which was one of the greatest best-sellers of its day, being reprinted more than fifty times. In this manifesto of eccentric geography, Donnelly propounded the basic tenets of neo-Atlantism:

- The lost continent was the source of all civilization, the biblical Garden of Eden, where early mankind dwelt in a state of idyllic peace and happiness.
- The gods and goddesses of the Egyptians, Greeks, Hindus, and Scandinavians were the rulers and heroes of ancient Atlantis.
- The Atlanteans colonized the Mediterranean, their most ancient colony being that in Egypt.
- The ancient civilizations of Mexico and Peru were also Atlantean colonies, and their sun-worshiping religion was the old, true religion of the mother country.
- Atlantis was destroyed in a terrible natural disaster, accurately reported by Plato, in which nearly everyone perished.
- Those few who escaped diffused civilization throughout the world, telling tales about the destruction of Atlantis, which were garbled and became the Deluge myths that form a part of nearly all mythologies in the world.

As is often the case with eccentric theories and their proponents, Donnelly argued from a negative posture: nothing can prove that I'm wrong. Nonetheless, he was persuasive. His books leave the casual lay reader with the impression that it could all have happened. Donnelly picked through the geological research of his era and discovered evidence for continents rising and sinking into the sea, though he took no cognizance of the fact that these events took place millions of years in the past, rather than 11,500 years ago. He detected resemblances between Old World and New World plants in an effort to show that Atlantis was the primeval motherland; he asserted that the Assyrians had pineapples, for example, and that tobacco once existed in the Old World.

Donnelly made sweeping linguistic claims, a distinctive feature of the eccentric Atlantists who would follow him. He tried to show a familial relationship between Mayan hieroglyphs and the Latin alphabet. Since the two look nothing whatever alike, he invented intermediate forms to bridge the gap. He asserted that the Chiapanec language of Mexico was closely related to Hebrew, and that Otomi, another Mexican language, resembled Chinese. Very little was known about the archaeology of the New World at that time—and absolutely nothing about ancient American languages—so Donnelly's sweeping assertions, bolstered with charts and engravings of lost temples, made a much better impression than his slipshod scholarship merited. Today, almost everything he wrote can be easily disproved: the Assyrian pineapples were conventional representations of date palms; his "tobacco" could have been hemp or any of a number of smokable herbs; the native languages of Mexico have not the slightest relationship to Hebrew or Chinese. His Chinese, in any case, is wildly off the mark.

Despite its many factual lapses, *Atlantis: The Antediluvian World* quickly became the bible of Atlantism, widely quoted by all subsequent theorists. Not one to let the grass grow underfoot, Donnelly went on to a political career with the Populist party, which he helped to found. He wrote several other books, including a futuristic novel called *Caesar's Column: A Story of the Twentieth Century,* which sold upward of a million copies, and *The Great Cryptogram,* which claimed to prove that Sir Francis Bacon, the Elizabethan poet and neo-Atlantist, wrote the plays of Shakespeare—yet another pseudoscholarly theory that launched a cult that has survived to this day. Even Sigmund Freud dabbled in such armchair historical revisionism, in his case a theory about ancient Egypt, and he got it no less wrong.

The Maya, mysterious builders of magnificent temples and cities, whose hieroglyphic language was not understood at all until the latter twentieth century, have provided a rich field for eccentric dreamers. One of the most imaginative of them was Auguste Le Plongeon (1826–1908), a French doctor who was the first systematic excavator of the remains of the Maya on the Yucatán peninsula. His greatest contribution was a series of beautiful, highly sophisticated photographs of the ruins, which are still among the best visual records of many sites. At Chichén Itzá, where he lived for many years, Le Plongeon discovered one of the most famous artworks of the Maya, a sculpture of the god Chacmool that is today the symbol of Mexican tourism, featured on thousands of travel posters.

It was the view of Le Plongeon and his wife, Alice, who was his constant collaborator, that Mayax, as he called the ancient kingdom of the Maya, was the source of all civilization, and that Atlantis was nothing more than a colony, the stepping-stone between the motherland and the primitive outback of Europe. To support his theories, Le Plongeon wrote "translations" of the hieroglyphic texts, colorful fables unaccompanied by any gloss or explanation of his methods.

The Le Plongeons chronicled the eventful life of Moo, queen of ancient Mayax, in a series of books written in a style somewhere between Ignatius T. T. Donnelly and Edgar Rice Burroughs. Queen Moo's brothers, the good Prince Coh and the evil Prince Aah, were rivals for her love. Moo married Coh, and Aah, inflamed with jealousy, murdered his brother. Moo built the temples of Chichén Itzá as funerary monuments for her slain husband, and fled, via Atlantis, to Egypt, where she was welcomed as the goddess Isis and founded the first Mediterranean civilization.

One of Le Plongeon's more outrageous claims was that the final words Jesus spoke on the cross were in the Mayan language. The Gospel of Matthew records them as *"Eli, Eli, lama sabachthani?,"* Aramaic for "My God, my God, why hast thou forsaken me?" Le Plongeon substituted for this, always one of the most puzzling verses of the New Testament, what he claimed was a phonetic version of Yucatec Maya: *"Hele, Hele, lamah zabac ta ni,"* which he translated as "Now, now I am fainting, darkness covers my face." It is exactly the sort of adventitious coincidence that the eccentric cherishes. It helped to ruin his reputation with reputable archaeologists and epigraphers: they may not have been able to understand ancient Mayan, but they knew it wasn't the language of Jesus.

Le Plongeon ended his life a broken man, his romantic theories utterly discredited. After his death, Alice Le Plongeon continued to propagate his ideas in a form that veered ever closer to, and finally arrived at, pulp fiction. From 1909 to 1911 she serialized a novel called *A Dream of Atlantis* in *The Word,* a magazine published by the Theosophical Society. She wrote that "a few years prior to the destruction of that famous land [Atlantis] a colony of the Old Maya stock again returned to the fatherland, in these days named Yucatán, and there founded a new empire," the one that built the impressive temples whose ruins are visible today. As her story progressed, romantic love affairs and epic battles occurred with regularity, now unencumbered by any attempt to connect them, however spuriously, with hieroglyphs.

As demented as the Le Plongeons' vision of Atlantis was, there was little doubt that they believed their own moonshine, always the mark of the true eccentric. More recent proponents of Atlantis, however, appear to be hoaxers, although their motives are often unclear and may also be tinged with eccentricity.

In 1912 Paul Schliemann, the grandson of Heinrich Schliemann, excavator of Troy and Mycenae, published an article in the *New York American* with the sensational title "How I Discovered Atlantis, the Source of All Civilization."

In this piece of egregious nonsense he claimed that his grandfather had bequeathed to him papers and a mysterious owl-headed vase that proved the existence of Atlantis. Inside the vase, he wrote, he found coins and a metal tablet with an inscription in Phoenician, which purportedly came from the lost continent. Young Schliemann corroborated his account with "translations" of Mayan manuscripts and an ancient Chaldean document, which he said came from Tibet—rather a long way from Chaldea. All these texts were obvious plagiarisms of Donnelly and Le Plongeon. Despite the transparency of Schliemann's hoax, he is frequently cited by modern Atlantists, no doubt because of the luster of his surname.

While Paul Schliemann was obviously a fraud, other cases are less clear, just as we cannot be entirely sure sometimes whether eccentric scientists really believe in the scientific validity of their perpetual-motion machines. Into this gray area falls James Churchward, an Anglo-American explorer (he later styled himself Colonel) and a friend of the Le Plongeons. Churchward was not satisfied with one lost continent; in addition to Atlantis, he propounded a second vanished continent in the Pacific, which he called Mu.

In a series of books beginning with *The Lost Continent of Mu,* in 1926, the colonel adduced the usual pseudoscience, nonscience, and antiscience to prove that Mu was the source of all human civilization and indeed of life itself, for Churchward disdained what he called the "monkey theories" of evolution. He dispensed with any attempt at an epigraphical proof of his theories, rather claiming to have a mystical ability to interpret all ancient symbols. If he stared at them long enough, he said, the hieroglyphs would "speak" to him in the language of their creators.

Mystical linguistic abilities are still a feature of eccentric lore: several of the eccentrics in our study claimed to have found meteorites from outer space, encoded with messages in unknown languages that they alone were able to decipher. One of them said she found her mystery rock on Sunset Strip, in Los Angeles; it was etched with a variety of hieroglyphics and Chinese characters.

In Churchward's visionary account of the Muvian language, the letter *M,* and therefore the symbol of the lost kingdom, was a rectangle. Not surprisingly, he was thus able to find evidence of Mu everywhere in the world. He gave his books the appearance of scientific treatises by adding charts and elegant maps, drawn and lettered in his own spidery hand, and justified the more fantastical statements with absurd footnotes such as "Greek record" and "Various records."

Churchward's postulation of a second sunken continent in addition to Atlantis, like almost everything else in his books, was a borrowing. Helena P. Blavatsky, the founder of the Theosophical Society, had already announced the existence of such a place, in her system called Lemuria, which spilled over from the Pacific into the Indian Ocean. With the occultism of Madame Blavatsky, we sail off into a Neverland that floats between the dreamers of golden ages, deviant geography and history, and eccentric religion. Madame Blavatsky was the estranged wife of a Russian general; she traveled around the world, supporting herself by working successively as a bareback rider, pianist, and medium, until she arrived in New York, where she founded the Theosophical Society in 1875.

Theosophy is an enormously complicated system, based upon Blavatsky's occult revelations. The science-fiction novelist L. Sprague De Camp, in *Lost Continents,* his definitive history of the subject, summarizes Blavatsky's cosmogony as

> a vast synthesis of Eastern and Western magic and myth about the seven planes of existence, the sevenfold cycles through which everything evolves, the seven Root Races of mankind, the seven bodies that each of us carries with him, and the Brotherhood of Mahatmas who run the world from headquarters in Tibet, by sending out streams of occult force and bustling about the world in their astral bodies.

The Lemurians, the third Root Race, began as egg-laying hermaphrodites with a third eye in the back of their heads (according to theosophists, the human pineal gland is the remnant of that third eye). After they discovered sex, the Lemurians interbred with beasts, thereby creating the apes. The arts of fire-making, metallurgy, and agriculture were all introduced to Lemuria by space travelers from the planet Venus, which already had a well-developed civilization. (We might suppose that Erich von Däniken had read his Blavatsky before he propounded his theory of the ancient astronauts who brought civilization to the earth.)

After the decline of Lemuria, Atlantis takes over with a bewildering series of subraces, increasingly bizarre in appearance, which were constantly involved in bloody wars against one another. Blavatsky's rather skeletal accounts of subracial strife in the antediluvian world were fleshed out in lurid detail by followers such as W. Scott-Elliot and Annie Besant, who succeeded her as leader of the Theosophical Society. In these extravagant fictions, history stretches back for millions of years, alchemy and astrology are facts of everyday life, and continents pop up and become submerged again with the clockwork regularity of carousel ponies.

It is incredible to think that such rubbish was ever taken seriously. It has been proved repeatedly that Blavatsky stole most of her occult visions from well-known Hindu scriptures such as the Rig Veda, and from earlier mystics and spiritualists such as Louis Jacolliot, who claimed to have found evidence in Sanskrit manuscripts for a sunken continent in the Indian Ocean, called Rutas, which was—what else?—the place where all civilization began. In 1884 the Society for Psychical Research declared Blavatsky a fraud, but that seems not to have deterred her followers, who, by the time of her death, numbered more than 100,000. Her writings and methods were the model for a myriad of "mystics." Alice Bailey produced dozens of books detailing *her* visions, and founded a cult called the Arcane School, which is still in existence. In the Baileyan universe, too, the Master resides in Tibet, but the civilizing race of superbeings comes not from Venus but from Neptune.

The occult had become a booming, if increasingly shady, business. Rival esoteric societies manufactured competitive Atlantean and Lemurian fantasies, all variations on themes that were becoming ever more predictable. Any con man who could afford the price of a comic-book advertisement could set up shop as a mystic, offering to share the wisdom of the ancients for a price. Even the American psychic healer and prophet Edgar Cayce had a stake in the Atlantis boom. He claimed to have direct contact with the floating souls of the former residents of Atlantis; further, he predicted that by the late 1960s remnants of the vanished continent would ascend above sea level, off the Bahamas. By this point, we are dealing not with eccentrics but with frauds; the true eccentric does not seek to deceive.

However, eccentric metaphysics is an irrepressible force in the human imagination, and it still continues to assert itself. Whereas Madame Blavatsky decked out her system of thought (if that's what it was) in the trappings of benevolent spiritualism, which was the fashion in her day, there exists a new cult of eccentric metaphysics that draws upon the contemporary fascination with communications technology. An international group called the Cercle d'Etudes sur la Transcommunication, based in Luxembourg, claims to be in direct communication with the dead, not via mediums in trances or Ouija boards but by computers and sophisticated electronic equipment. The CETL reports that a group of dead scientists in a parallel world called Varid are collaborating on a system to communicate with the living people of Earth. These messages take the form of telephone calls, computer transmissions, and video pictures, which are published in the group's publications.

The leader of the dead scientists is Dr. Swejen Salter (1949–87), who runs what is called the TimeStream Sending

Station, in Varid. In one of her phone calls, Salter describes her death experience:

> I died at the age of thirty-eight as the result of an accident. Death came suddenly and unexpected. I was totally unprepared and cannot remember my passing over. I awoke on a recliner in a cheerfully decorated room that I had never seen before. Before I could have a closer look around, a tall, imposing man entered the room and identified himself as Richard Francis Burton. He welcomed me and started showing me the world in which he had lived since the year 1890 of your earth time. I felt happy and safe here. Everybody was friendly and helpful. Still, the change was difficult. It is not easy to adapt to a new life when one is torn away from a daily routine.

Sir Richard Burton (1821–90), discoverer of Lake Tanganyika and translator of the *Arabian Nights,* is Swejen Salter's constant companion on the spirit side. In the summer of 1988, the year after she died, she and Burton traveled aboard the *Thrakka,* a spaceship built by the TimeStream group, to a planet called Marduk. The anonymous writer of the CETL publication tells his readers that "the description of their travels, given over radio and telephone, reads like a science-fiction story." The video pictures that accompanied this fascinating travelogue were received on a broken television set, which the writer stresses as a proof of their authenticity.

Salter has met a number of famous dead scientists, who told her that they would collaborate with her in the great work of perfecting transcommunication technology; both Marie Curie and Albert Einstein have promised to help. Others have refused, including Alexander Graham Bell. "I regret his refusal," said Swejen Salter. "Mr. Bell could have been of great help in improving our telephone contacts."

Salter marshals impressive-sounding scientific jargon to support her descriptions of the afterlife. Here are a few passages from her explanation of why people on the spirit side don't age, from a computer message sent on May 14, 1988, to the main CETL receiving laboratory in Luxembourg:

> The relevant parameters of ageing can be plotted in three quasi-dimensions as a changing spiral. An organism begins life by reproduction on the broad base line. It develops along the time line with a constant gradient, spiraling upward, and grows into a conical shape to a point indicating the individual's death. Contrary to a straight endless (infinite) line, the cyclic windings of the spiral correspond to the cyclic effects of the internal-external environment, such as annual effects.

> Due to the speed of retrocession, your [i.e., in the living world] laboratory signals are subject to a transfinite red shift and arrive with zero energy. The problem you have with the future is that it does not yet exist for you.

> I know you have many questions, and I am trying to answer them as well as possible. But it will largely have to remain theory. Mankind simply does not have the necessary fundamentals yet, neither spiritual nor physical. Several elements such as fermium and the Hahn particle have not yet been discovered on Terra, contrary to Planet Varid. How

shall I give you instructions for building an apparatus when several metals do not even exist?

Of course, this pseudoscientific blather, so much like bad dialogue from a pulp science-fiction novel or a 1950s flying-saucer movie, has the unmistakable odor of fraud clinging to it. Where there is no pecuniary motive, we must look for fun as the motive. Undergraduate smart alecks have been confounding their elders with hoaxes for centuries. The message from Swejen Salter quoted above appeared in a computer file belonging to a transcommunication researcher in Luxembourg named Ernst Senkowski Mainz. The question is, who put it there?

A good proportion of computer hackers are eccentric, including several of the subjects in the study. Because of their innate ability to innovate and their penchant for the unorthodox, many young science jocks are able to live a solitary, nocturnal life, devising complex computer programs. It is exactly the sort of culture that might breed the Swejen Salter myth. Yet even if the message was put into the computer by a hacker-jokester, for educated scientists and technicians, which the members of the CETL plausibly claim to be, to devote their lives and careers to such a bizarrerie might well be a symptom of eccentricity.

The question of whether the recipients of Swejen Salter's messages are sincere in their professions of belief in their authenticity is another imponderable subjectivity: they *seem* to believe in it, and it is difficult to see what motive there might be in pretending to believe. Unless, like Toto pulling back the curtain to reveal the Wizard of Oz at his levers, we catch them in the act, typing in fake messages signed "Swejen Salter," we have no reason to suppose that they are insincere in their professions. And even if they are inventing the whole thing, is their myth-making essentially different from that of Plato in his writings about Atlantis? Everyone dreams; it is the eccentrics among us who sometimes fail to distinguish between the dream world and waking reality.

SIX

Eccentricity and Mental Illness

Had there been a lunatic asylum in the suburbs of Jerusalem, Jesus Christ would infallibly have been shut up in it at the outset of his public career. That interview with Satan on a pinnacle of the Temple would alone have damned him, and everything that happened after could but have confirmed the diagnosis.

—*Havelock Ellis,*
Impressions and Comments

THROUGHOUT THE STUDY, MY RESEARCHERS AND I MADE A CONTINUous effort to distinguish between eccentricity and the forms of mental illness that mimic it. Nonetheless, eccentrics do not have any special immunity from mental illness. Logic dictates that eccentrics, original and excessive in every other field of life, must surely exhibit some extravagant strains of mental illness. Yet we found that it was no easy

136

matter to clarify the line of demarcation between eccentricity and mental illness.

In the first place, there were few precedents to guide us. Formerly, the terms "eccentricity" and "madness" were used almost interchangeably to describe anyone whose behavior was strange and unpredictable. Early Freudian psychiatrists focused on the unbridgeable gulf between those who were clearly ill and the rest of us. They believed in the maxim "Even a touch of schizophrenia is still schizophrenia," and labeled milder conditions as borderline disorders. Because eccentricity itself did not quite fit into classic psychiatric diagnoses, some early theorists mistakenly thought of it as a psychological "missing link" between normality and serious thought disorders or personality disorders.

Modern psychiatrists are no less confused than their predecessors on the subject of eccentricity. As the number of possible diagnoses of mental illness grows, so does the possibility of erroneous classification. Most psychiatrists and psychologists have very little direct experience with eccentric people. A psychiatrist may meet only a few eccentrics in his entire career, and then only under unusual circumstances. Modern eccentrics are deft at avoiding admission to mental hospitals. Undoubtedly they do sometimes come under psychiatric care, but since the mental-health establishment is overwhelmingly geared toward identifying and treating diseases, a diagnosis of harmless eccentricity, even when it might be obvious, goes against the grain. Like the traffic cop who is rewarded for issuing as many tickets as possible, psychiatrists and psychologists are far more likely to find illness than benign conditions that do not require treatment—much less behavior that deserves positive encouragement.

In one large teaching hospital in Britain, over a ten-year period only 2 out of 23,350 patients received at discharge a primary diagnosis of eccentric personality. One was admitted briefly for a sleep problem, which had nothing to do with her eccentricity. The second, a twenty-one-year-old university dropout, was admitted because a volunteer counselor did not know what to make of him, although he suspected schizophrenia. The diagnosis of eccentricity in this patient's case seemed to be based upon a comment his mother made to the examining psychiatrist: "When I get depressed, I wonder what I have done to have such eccentric children, but when I'm well I feel glad that they have such individuality." The patient discharged himself against medical advice after less than three full days in the hospital.

Such a preposterously low number of diagnoses indicates that, for all practical purposes, as far as modern medicine is concerned eccentricity does not exist. Even if a psychiatrist were fairly sure of his ground in identifying eccentricity, it is still likely that the patient would receive some other label, usually that of a common mental illness. That may be the result not only of the widely acknowledged unreliability of psychiatric diagnosis but also of the perceived need among doctors to communicate with one another in an esoteric jargon that reflects shared perspectives and expectations—hence the frequently observed phenomenon that certain illnesses seem to go in and out of fashion. These considerations may in turn be derived from hierarchical power relationships and career motivations. There is pressure on mental health professionals, as on workers in every field, to agree with their superiors and provide them with data to prove their theories.

Yet we still have not confronted the crucial question: do eccentrics share any of the core characteristics of the genuinely mentally disturbed? In order to answer this question, we carried out standard investigations for the possible presence of various forms of so-called first-rank and second-rank symptoms of schizophrenia and other signs of thought disorder among the eccentrics.

To do this, we used the same primary interview technique used by our psychiatric colleagues, the mental-state examination. The most reliable and widely recognized version is the Present State Examination (PSE), a series of carefully worded questions designed to elicit the symptoms of mental illness. This test has been in wide use for more than twenty years, in interviews with several hundred thousand people, and it is still evolving and improving. Its extensive use has shown to what extent the variability in making a psychiatric diagnosis, which is due to the subjective elements in defining, recognizing, and classifying symptoms, can be rendered in a more objective form.

The PSE is a semistructured interview with suggested probes for each symptom. It covers a subject's symptoms during the previous four weeks, as well as abnormalities of speech and behavior during the interview itself. We also asked about similar experiences in the preceding six months, thus anchoring any such symptoms to events that could be dated. In addition, other questions in our own interviews were posed in such a way that we could draw out abnormal symptoms that had occurred anytime in the eccentrics' lives.

Each symptom is rated on a three- or four-point scale. A detailed manual gives definitions of the symptoms to be rated, and indicates the level of severity required for each point of the scale. Several of the questions in the PSE concern the obvious symptoms of schizophrenia—visual and auditory hallucinations, and various types of delusions. Other questions are derived from a system devised by the German psychiatrist Kurt Schneider, who has distinguished ten symptoms of schizophrenia that he classifies as first-rank.

1. Hearing one's own thoughts spoken aloud.

2. Hallucinatory voices in the form of statement and reply. The subject hears voices speaking about him in the third person.

3. Hallucinatory voices in the form of a running commentary.

4. Bodily hallucinations. The subject has sensations in his body that he believes are produced by external agencies.

5. Thought withdrawal. The subject believes that his thoughts are taken out of his head, as though a person or external force were removing them.

6. Thought insertion. The subject believes that thoughts are being put into his head that are not his own.

7. Thought broadcasting. The subject feels that his thoughts are being broadcast, so that other people know what he is thinking.

8. Thought blocking. The stream of conscious thought becomes disordered; a gap appears in a sequence of thought. The subject will pause abruptly, and when he speaks again he goes off on a tangent, like a tape recording with a blank space arbitrarily cut out of it.

9. Delusional perception. An abnormal meaning, usually of a self-referencing nature, is attributed to a normal perception without any logical reason. For example, a patient (not an eccentric) heard a neighbor bang a door, and she was instantly convinced that this signified that she was being systematically persecuted, without a shred of objective evidence to confirm any malevolent intent.

10. Any events in the realms of feelings, motivations, and free will that are experienced as having been manufactured or influenced by others.

Although Schneider's first-rank symptoms are useful for stringently defining the core of schizophrenia, their diagnostic value is questionable, for they are primarily symptoms of severe breakdown. However, because they refer to specific, primarily verbal expressions that most people would find too bizarre to encompass in a model of healthy human nature, they also possess an enduring face validity. They have stood up well against the test of time, and have helped to distinguish schizophrenia and paranoid psychosis from other mental illnesses.

The originator of the theory behind these first-rank symptoms is the shadowy, tragic figure of Victor Tausk (1879–1919), who had an intuitive ability to grasp the inner turmoil in the minds of the disturbed. He was the first member of

the Vienna Psychoanalytic Society to study psychoses clinically, at a time when Sigmund Freud himself was interested
only in treating much less disordered people. Tausk was the
first to describe the concept of the loss of ego boundaries,
the schizophrenic's belief that everyone else knows what
he is thinking, that his thoughts are not enclosed within his
own mind but are spread throughout the world and occur
simultaneously in the minds of other people. When suffering from this condition, the person is no longer able to
realize that he is a separate psychological entity. In someone with paranoid tendencies, the loss of ego boundaries
could, for instance, be translated into the belief that other
people are stealing his ideas.

It is bitterly ironic that, for at least six years, Freud and
Tausk were acutely aware of each other's originality, to the
point where they both may have wondered who was borrowing ideas from whom, and both became concerned
about the issue of scientific precedence before that was a
widespread problem. Eventually they felt inhibited in each
other's company, lest one of them give away an important
idea to the other.

During the eccentricity project, we placed special emphasis on uncovering thought disorders by looking for PSE
symptoms that pointed to their existence. The main reason
for doing this was because eccentricity has been mentioned
by some researchers as a cardinal feature of schizophrenia
in people predisposed to schizophrenia though not necessarily suffering from it, and in schizoid personality disorder.
Moreover, in every study since the beginning of this century, the most common trait found in the well, nonpsychotic

relatives of schizophrenic patients has been some forms of eccentric behavior.

We stood this on its head and wondered if symptoms that turned up frequently in schizophrenics might not be found in the eccentrics. Such an exercise would show if there was more than a merely circumstantial relationship between the two conditions. It might well have been the case that although schizophrenics are eccentric, at least according to a dictionary definition, the converse need not apply. The crucial test was to ascertain the frequency and severity of characteristic first-rank schizophrenic symptoms among eccentrics, using the questions and criteria laid out in the PSE. Our results were tangible proof that the mental life of the eccentric is unlike anything that psychology has yet described.

Symptoms commonly associated with schizophrenia were prevalent in the eccentric sample, albeit in mild form. The one exception was thought insertion, which did not occur at all. Every subject in the project, with typical eccentric egocentricity, believed that all his thoughts were uniquely and originally his own. It was the first time that these symptoms have been detected to such an extent in any sample population taken directly from the community, however unorthodox the sample.

However, it ought not to be deduced from that that schizophrenia runs rampant in the eccentric population. In fact, as we shall see, studies have shown that it may actually be somewhat less prevalent than in the general population. In Table 6.1, the middle column, labeled "partial/mild," reflects symptoms that could never result in a diagnosis of

TABLE 6.1:

Frequency of PSE Symptoms of Schizophrenia (%)

Symptom	Absent	Partial/Mild	Full/Severe
Delusion of thought being read	62	38	0
Thought insertion	100	0	0
Thought broadcast	94	5	1
Thought block	70	29	1
Delusions of alien forces controlling the mind	88	11	1
Auditory hallucinations	70	25	5
Visual hallucinations	65	26	9
Delusional misinterpretation	69	26	5
Delusions of persecution	57	41	2
Religious delusions	55	41	4
Paranormal delusions	70	27	3

schizophrenia, but which are rather isolated instances of such phenomena. More than anything else, the high numbers in some of the categories show the extent to which the extraordinarily vivid imagination of eccentrics verges on the visionary.

The second, even more significant finding was that although a high proportion of the sample showed one or more of these symptoms to a mild or partial degree, only one individual had a full-blown psychosis during the interview. Simon, a British man of fifty-eight, possessed many of the cardinal symptoms of paranoid schizophrenia and pronounced delusions of grandeur. Any decent psychiatrist would have recognized him as being ill within five minutes. The following excerpt from Simon's interview shows not only how he talks about himself, but also how straightforward and clear the diagnostic process can be when using the PSE:

> To Monty, I was better known as the Chief Scout of the British Army. Captured Cicero . . . took British invasion plans, then changed them to suit us. History books all lie, saying that Britain was invincible. By becoming German, I literally killed Rommel, outclassed General von Rundstedt. Directed the British in the Battle of the Bulge even before it happened. [Uncontrollable laughter.] No one has shot me yet! So keeping out of the limelight line of sight has proved without doubt using one's own initiative and mind. No stupid spy story's ideas, cannot catch you out with letters, phone-tapping, meeting people, reading papers, but they only know the name of the grandson of General . . . No one knows where he is. He sends funny postcards to the government telling them openly what's going to happen. News for everybody!

The fact that out of the entire sample we had only one such episode of full-blown psychosis argues in favor of the proposition that there is no direct link between eccentricity and mental illness. Moreover, recent evidence has shown that the prevalence of abnormal psychiatric symptoms in ostensibly normal populations is exceedingly high—considerably higher, indeed, than the incidence of mild symptoms in our eccentric sample.

One study at the University of California found constellations of mild to moderate symptoms among undergraduates at Berkeley occurring at a rate of 15 percent, an estimate that has been borne out by other studies. Our eccentric group, on the other hand, showed an overall rate of 8 percent at an equivalent degree of severity. The eccentrics who constituted that 8 percent were not necessarily ill, but rather exhibited strikingly unusual thought processes. In many cases the strange thinking pattern was adopted deliberately, and was quite comprehensible in the appropriate context. Most important, it was functional rather than dysfunctional, and more often than not it was praised and rewarded.

Occurring more commonly in this study were the kinds of minimal delusional beliefs that most people would be more likely to regard as normal irrationality rather than as delusions. Religious and paranormal delusions, for example, might be more commonly described as superstition. Astrology has no basis in science, and is in fact completely irrational, yet belief in it is widespread. If we were to classify all the people who read their horoscope in the morning paper as borderline schizophrenics, we would need to recruit a million new psychiatrists to transform all of them into uniformly rational people. But who would ever want to do that?

Admittedly, astrology is a mild example of an irrational belief system. Some of our eccentrics believed in paranormal phenomena that were far more bizarre. One man claimed that he saw ghosts: "I see . . . figures. Not every day of the week. I have run after figures, absolutely bonkers, and then I discover when I look back through history books that Lady So-and-so stayed in that same room in the castle, and she had seen a specter on the hill, and so on, so I hadn't imagined it after all." Another subject told us that she had intensely unpleasant intuitive reactions whenever she was on the site of a battlefield or a place where a violent crime had taken place.

When we asked the eccentrics how they came by such extraordinary ideas, or why they harbored such beliefs, their immediate answer was usually in the form of "evidence," derived from a hallucinatory experience (one man told us, "Because many of the departed ask me for help") or from near-death experiences. Here is a detailed account by a forty-eight-year-old woman of her epiphany:

> I was on the correct side of the road, not traveling very fast, and this furniture van is going very fast down the hill. We were inside a forty-mile-an-hour limit. He couldn't take the corner, and he came right at me. I was in a compact car with the furniture van coming right at me, and I just sat there terrified for less than a second, and then I thought, "I know this is it, this is it." I said to myself, "This is the end of everything." The next question that came into my mind was, "I wonder what happens next," and at that moment it was almost as if I had left the car—I don't feel I was in the car

seat any more. I was in an absolutely strange sort of ecstasy. It is terribly difficult to describe, but I seemed to be merged—it was as if I had almost disappeared. I seemed to be merged with everything else in a marvelous ecstasy.

Eccentric paranormal and religious delusions usually place a great emphasis on the forces of harmony, nature, and a cosmic order that cannot be expressed in mere words. These forces are doing battle with and finally vanquishing society's claims upon the individual to lead a conventional, humdrum existence devoid of idealism. This approach has been described as promethean. In promethean individuals, there is an ordering of values that accepts, and believes in, the necessity for change. They are guided by an overmastering desire to remake the world according to their own enlightened and often misunderstood precepts. Beethoven, for example, has been identified as being of this type.

Some theorists have characterized the messianic dedication of such people as "an attempt to deal with extreme feelings of worthlessness," but this was not the case with our eccentric subjects. In addition to their principal motivation of wishing to save mankind, the earth, or portions thereof, they also stressed the value of heightened self-awareness, insight, and a deep sympathy with all living things. Yet they did not repudiate the desire to control other people. This class of eccentrics is not very receptive or responsive to other people, and they usually prefer to do their good works, or to enrich their inner life, in solitude. They are equally able to abstain from, or enthusiastically partake of, what one of them called "earthly delights and pleasures."

Schizophrenia itself might begin with the development of a false reality. Objective facts cannot always be distinguished from subjective intuitions, even by ordinary, well people. Thus under certain circumstances a person's grasp of reality may be made to feel false, or at least be thrown into question and subtly invalidated. It has been said, uncharitably, that while neurotics construct castles in the air, psychotics live in them. This formula is not only unkind: it is wrong. It overlooks the essential role played by fantasy in human affairs.

Normal people, and eccentrics even more so, use imagination so much in their everyday lives that it becomes a kind of silent partner in their inner lives, seldom thought about consciously yet absolutely essential. We become oblivious to how much of our planning, predictive ability, memory, and foresight depend upon our imaginative processes. The power of the imagination becomes apparent to us only when our attention is drawn to these related skills. When they are talked about concretely they can sound absurd, but behind the seeming absurdity there may be something valuable—or perhaps something sinister. Here is an account from one eccentric, a twenty-five-year-old man named Peter, about the construction of his alternative reality. It is quoted in full, because it provides an excellent example of a large-scale, highly detailed delusion:

I have produced a fictitious Secondary World in response to living in the real one. This Secondary World does not set out to transport its inventor to a time or place far removed from the frightening realities of contemporary techno-society by conjuring up the conventional elements of myth. Rather, it is a place I model firmly on present world realities. It's a place in which reflected versions of elements of the real world are carefully exaggerated, so that by imagining them as if they were real, their impact upon me would be greater. As a bonus, the Secondary World serves me by interpreting and predicting events in the real one.

There is one element of the Secondary World that would immediately identify me as an eccentric, and that is my constant use of props. The principal ones are architectural: miniature models of buildings, all kinds of them, set among streets, playgrounds, light poles, and the like. Everything is constructed as exactly to scale as I can make it. I move toy cars in and out of driveways and use model trucks to replicate such occurrences as fuel deliveries and garbage collection, all on a regular schedule.

The weather plays an enormous role in this. When it is inclement outside I use small fans to engineer appropriate equivalents of strong winds. I introduce rain by reproducing its general sound in my own ears at the proper rate, allowing my breath to be expelled through my partially closed lips. I produce a low hissing or rushing sound which I control in its quality and intensity in accordance with the actual rain outside. Meanwhile, I constantly project detailed mental images onto the set, mimicking the quantity and patterns of wetness, as if I were seeing real buildings and streets made wet in the course of a rainy day or night.

The number of areas of concern in the Secondary World

is large, because I feel involved in, and affected by, a large number of things in the real world. They include governments, corporations and industrial concerns, large man-made objects (ships, aircraft, weapons, etc.), local surroundings, and various large-scale, deep trends and tendencies in the world's social complexion. All of this requires an extensive, exhaustive support structure of quality maps at various scales to describe the Secondary World in detail. It demands tremendous commitment and dedication from me. As you might guess, I am extremely busy.

Peter's fantasy life, clearly, has taken over. Most psychiatrists would leap at the chance to diagnose and cure him. Yet while his Secondary World might seem to a dispassionate, noneccentric observer to be a pathetic waste of time, or a neurotic attempt to escape from life, there is no compelling reason to believe that his life would be improved by dissuading him from his chosen profession, that of caretaker of a parallel universe. Just because it is imaginary, like Norton's empire, does not mean that his life would be enhanced by giving it up. The fact that other people cannot understand the Secondary World in no way invalidates its rewards for Peter.

Peter also told us that he was lonely and had trouble making friends. Unlike the majority of eccentrics in the project, he was not a happy person. Yet life carries with it no guarantee of being happy: plenty of normal, healthy people have unhappy lives. Notice how clearly, intelligently, and forcefully Peter presented his Secondary World to the interviewer: even though he devotes his life to the caretaking of an illusion, he is no schizophrenic. He has simply organized his life along a particularly strange set of alternative coordinates.

While Peter does not demand that other people believe in his Secondary World, many delusionary eccentrics do impose upon, and strain, the credulity of the world. The specific claims they make, which may be their way of attempting to reconcile the irreconcilable within themselves, often sound incredible and absurd. Yet attempts to construe such quasi-logical beliefs as symptoms of mild mental illness are never quite convincing: symptoms on their own do not constitute a syndrome, and still less can one or even a few isolated beliefs be made to constitute a diagnosis of illness.

Only one subject had a clear psychosis at the time of the interview, Simon, the man who killed Rommel and fought the Battle of the Bulge before it happened. Judging from the evidence of his presentation, he had been in an advanced state of delusional disintegration for a long while, yet as far as we know he had never received any treatment for his condition. No one in his close-knit mining village community realized that anything was amiss with him. But at the interview, in a state of massive thought disorder, he attempted to authenticate his claim to be a modern James Bond by demonstrating the commando throat-cutting drill, using my research associate Kate Ward as the surprised "enemy" victim.

Another revelation was that while 36 percent of the sample could detail a family history of overt eccentric behavior, the rate of mental illness among their relatives was only very slightly higher than that of the general population, a variation within a tolerable margin of error. Three middle-aged subjects, two male and one female, each had sons who were schizophrenic; another woman had a mother who had suffered a single episode of manic-depressive psychosis. These four were the only eccentric subjects who had a first-degree relative positively diagnosed for a serious psychiatric disorder. Three other eccentric subjects, two men and one woman, had second-degree relatives with serious mental disorders, two of whom were diagnosed as schizophrenic. The remaining subject had at least four relatives with pathological depression.

By comparison, however, the relatives of schizophrenics are far more likely to suffer from serious mental illness than are the relatives of eccentrics. Furthermore, while studies of schizophrenic patients have shown that they have a much greater chance of having first-degree relatives who display eccentric behavior than do mentally healthy people, it doesn't work the other way around. People who call themselves eccentric do not have an increased proportion of first-degree relatives with schizophrenia or other psychoses. At the same time, there is also a vastly increased likelihood—one in three for eccentrics, as opposed to approximately one in a thousand for noneccentrics—that the individual has a relative who is eccentric. It is usually a grandparent, an aunt or uncle, or a more distant relative.

This finding is very hard to explain. The implied relationship between schizophrenia and eccentricity can be disposed of easily. In the first place, the eccentric behavior of schizophrenics and their relatives may be qualitatively different from that of eccentrics who are leading happy, well-adjusted lives, like most of the subjects in the study. It is also possible that psychiatrists who are treating or researching schizophrenia may have a lower threshold for what constitutes eccentric behavior than most people do. They are trained to be in a constant state of readiness to notice abnormal mannerisms and speech. However, the great majority of psychiatrists have never, or very rarely, met healthy, happy eccentrics, and they have certainly never studied them in depth, a fact proved negatively by the absence of any significant published record.

It might be inferred, therefore, that eccentrics do not share a family relationship in any sense with schizophrenics, and that any perceived similarities are simply coincidental, by dint of their oddness. It is difficult, though not impossible, to categorize different types of odd behavior: aside from being statistically infrequent, they are also all different from one another.

We had assumed at the beginning of the study that it was unlikely that we would find any eccentrics married to each other or living together. In the first place, there was the statistical rarity: if our estimate of one in 10,000 was even roughly correct, given the reclusiveness of many eccentrics the odds seemed to be against them even meeting one another. Furthermore, it seemed almost impossible that someone who had spent most of his or her life becoming idiosyncratic would be attracted to someone else with an altogether different collection of hobbyhorses. Yet the study proved these assumptions to be wrong or, at best, premature.

ECCENTRICS

We discovered no fewer than three couples with both partners equally eccentric. Two other female subjects said that their husbands were eccentric, but the latter were unavailable for the research interview. If we accept those two unverified cases, that yields odds of an eccentric-eccentric marriage, based on our British sample, of 1 in 26. The number seemed much too low, but there it was. These five couples have produced a total of seven children, all but one of whom are still too young to be considered for the study. The one child who is now in early adult life is a young man who has reacted by becoming extremely conservative and trying to be as normal as possible.

The children of these eccentric-eccentric marriages will be interesting to watch, for they may help us to make some preliminary judgments about the possible causes of eccentricity. If there are any predisposing genes for the condition, these children will inherit them, and their family environment abounds in good examples of eccentric behavior. Alternatively, it may be that there is little genetic transmission, and that the high proportion of eccentrics with eccentric relatives simply indicates that it is learned behavior. Perhaps contact with an eccentric uncle or grandmother may serve as an example that one can lead a different way of life, and bend the twig in a nonconformist direction.

This environmental explanation has its complications, too; despite the fact that a large majority of the eccentric subjects had children, very few of them have as yet shown any signs of eccentricity whatsoever. It appears that most of the children of eccentrics have reacted against it, such as the young conservative whose parents are both eccentric. Like the child of the alcoholic who loathes the very smell of wine, these children develop a determination to become as conventional as possible. Eccentricity of the enduring kind, it would appear, may develop and come to fruition only under rather special circumstances.

SEVEN

Eccentric Childhood

Probably all education is but two things: first, the parrying of
the ignorant children's impetuous assault on the truth, and
second, the gentle, imperceptible, step-by-step initiation of
the humiliated children into the Lie.

—*Franz Kafka*

ECCENTRICITY IS AT LEAST PARTLY A MATTER OF CHOICE, A CHOICE
that usually requires considerable bravery. That holds true
particularly at the point where eccentric behavior begins.
All of us have experienced a moment when we stood out
from the crowd, being inappropriately dressed or espous-
ing an opinion contrary to everyone else's, and know that
awful, lonely feeling of seeing the whole world lined up
against us. Eccentrics revel in that feeling. It becomes second nature to them. Yet in the beginning, the fledgling
eccentric risks ridicule and ostracism without having expe-

rienced the positive, pleasurable sensations that his differentness may, and usually will, bring him eventually.

We discovered that at least two-thirds of the eccentrics in the study knew by the age of eight that they were different from everybody else, though in many cases they kept that knowledge to themselves for years, until they felt confident enough to express it. Women were more likely than men to keep their eccentricity to themselves until they were adults. Eccentrics share this secretiveness with intellectually gifted children, who conceal the full scope of their powers so that they will not be thought of as odd and thus be rejected or taken advantage of. The eccentric science-fiction writer Isaac Asimov recalled the moment he became aware of the fact that he was different:

> When I was six years old, I was standing on the corner gazing up at the sky during a snowstorm. I was watching the snowflakes, which were dark against the clouds but instantly turned white when they moved downwards against the buildings. My mother called me into the house and lectured me endlessly, to the effect that I must cease my peculiar behavior. As I grew older, however, I came to be viewed as an unusual person in a complimentary sense.

It is hard to determine at exactly what point in a child's development that sort of self-consciousness emerges. Until they are six to eight years old, most children lack the intellectual sophistication to be able to compare their personality attributes and abilities with those of other children. They engage in simpler comparisons, with parents, teachers, and other adults. Psychologists have found that conformity normally increases during the middle childhood years, as the pressure to socialize—Kafka's "step-by-step initiation into the Lie"—mounts steadily.

The primary pressure to conform comes from the family, through the concentration of authority and power in the hands of two loving, benevolent people who have, absolutely, the last word. Parents want their children to be normal, to grow up to be good adults according to the values and mores of their society. Children are usually brought up to fear instability and change, and to desire the comfort of solid order and firmly structured routines. Few young children can conceptualize the consequences of their actions, not because of their age or developmental stage but mostly because of the way they are treated. Some families inculcate dependency and helplessness, especially in girls, who have been shown to be more conforming to peer-group pressures than boys are.

One of the first trends we discovered from our statistical analysis of the sample was that there was a marked preponderance of firstborn children, slightly more than 70 percent. Firstborn children have always enjoyed a position of privilege in the great majority of the world's cultures: among nomads, hunter-gatherers, and agricultural groups, as well as traditionally literate, politically sophisticated societies such as those of India and China.

In addition, every variety of family system values the firstborn, whether the line of descent is traced through the father's family or the mother's family, or where both lineages are given equal weight. In some societies, the procreation of the firstborn child is considered to be a religious duty, and in others it is believed that the birth of a first child confers immortality on the parents. In ancient Hebrew law, a firstborn child who was also the oldest surviving offspring was entitled to a double portion of the father's estate; in traditional Polynesian law, the chief was a firstborn from a line of firstborns.

Folk belief, custom and tradition, legal controls, and ordinary day-to-day family practices merge to demonstrate the significance of being a firstborn child. Studies have also shown a preponderance of firstborns among university students and among eminent scientists. However, many such children become overly conscientious and conformist. Sometimes the birth of a sibling can act as a goad, or a source of endless jealousy and rivalry, to the firstborn.

When a sibling enters the family, there is first the shock of what Alfred Adler termed the "dethronement." The behavior of both parents toward the firstborn changes after the birth of the second child. The firstborn is no longer the epicenter of his parents' attention, and he may temporarily be given a lower priority. Firstborn children then develop power tactics in their relations with the new sibling, whom they often provoke to the point of aggression. Firstborn children will continue to strive to maintain a high profile and be visibly different from the competitor for their parents' affections. This can make them more compulsively demanding, and can sometimes direct them toward idiosyncratic ambitions. Things can go sourly awry at this stage. One eccentric woman in the study described her relations with her siblings, an account that gives a new dimension to the concept of the brat:

We were all going to the zoo, and my sister was downstairs, crying. I had seen my father pacify my mother when she was upset by giving her a cigarette, and it crossed my mind that the same thing might work for my sister. I found a packet and tried to get a cigarette into her mouth. My mother thought I was trying to choke her, and then my father beat me so severely with a golf club that I could hardly walk. What angered me was the unfairness of it. From then on it became a battle of wits between my father and me, and I cared nothing at all for my mother. I regarded my sister as alien to me. My main priority was *space*—I insisted on my own bedroom, and got it by terrorizing my sister until she showed intense distress at being left alone with me. Antisocial behavior served me well.

By the time I was twelve I had the upper hand. My family feared me more than I feared them. In order not to be left with the thankless task of child-caring, I developed a habit of "nonremembering"—specifically not remembering where I left my sister, and abandoning the baby carriage and its contents in various places. Discerning that mama did not like tramps, I assiduously cultivated them, and acquired some useful nonstandard education in the process. I was habitually alone in the house without supervision. One afternoon I went out and met a tramp, and invited him home for tea. I made tea for him, using the best tea service. My mother came back while this was going on and was pretty annoyed, especially about the tea service.

By the age of seven or eight, children are usually able to understand the notion of similarity and difference vis-à-vis their own and others' personalities. Their motivation to make social comparisons between themselves and others begins to become apparent as early as four years of age, and reaches a peak between seven and nine years. It was at this age that most eccentrics, at least two-thirds of our sample, realized or were told that they were different. How this happened, why they felt it, and how they acted upon it is almost invariably a defining moment in the life of the eccentric.

It can begin simply by happenstance. One British woman in the study was a child during World War II. When she was evacuated from London during the Blitz to stay with her grandmother, she attended school in the village, where she began to learn to write. The next year, her grandmother moved, and when she was again evacuated to stay with her, the school in the new village used a different kind of writing paper, with extra lines printed to help the children form their letters. "So I said, 'Please, Miss, can I write on ordinary lines?' All the other children sniggered, and the teacher insisted that I should learn to write all over again, like the others." She now believes that this early experience of the tyrannical arbitrariness of the society at her school pointed her in the direction of eccentricity.

Sometimes a chance meeting can trigger it. Another Englishwoman reported that a single remark, said with conviction, touched off a lifetime of eccentricity: "There was an elderly couple living near us at Bath. They were spiritualists. One day the woman put her hand on my head and said to my parents, 'Your child is truly psychic.' Although I didn't know what the word meant, I remember feeling that it marked me as being different."

A third woman in the study told us that she decided at the age of seven that she was different from everyone else because of her name, Salome: "I made a decision that, having an unusual name, I was damn well going to be different."

In some cases, gender confusion provided the instigatory influence. The parents of some eccentrics treated them in childhood as though they would have preferred them to be of the opposite sex. This led to gender confusion, though it actually caused androgynous feelings more often than homosexual or bisexual orientations. These statements, from an eccentric woman and man respectively, illustrate how childhood gender confusion can help to launch an eccentric life:

I was not a typical girl. I was brought up as a boy. When my father came back from the war he was absolutely delighted because I was interested in and could do all the things he wanted to do. I was brought up to think and act like and just be a boy. I enjoyed it. I wouldn't have swapped it. I still enjoy shooting and fishing.

The difficulty I had, from the age of two, was in meeting my father's exacting, and totally misguided, standards of normality with regard to what was appropriate boyish behavior. To please him I would have had to display complete imperviousness to my mother's influence. Indeed, I would have had to be more disobedient than I had any inclination to be.

Most eccentrics experienced prolonged periods of isolation in their childhoods, either the result of being ostracized by their peers on account of their differentness, or because of circumstances, in which case the period of isolation often contributed to the development of their eccentricity. During these episodes they fell back on their own resources for amusement and solace, and experimented with their solitary surroundings. These pastimes became intrinsically rewarding and absorbing, and removed them still further from a normal childhood. One woman who grew up in Texas, near the NASA space center, was obsessed with outer space:

> Did I mention my Martian friend? From about the age of eight I had an imaginary friend from Mars. I still wonder sometimes if he was perhaps real after all. Being right there during the space race contributed to it. Good grief, we had Scott Carpenter over for dinner one night. He gave me a ten-inch model of the Mercury capsule. I escaped to my fantasy world on Mars frequently. From the age of eight to fourteen, I spent more time on Mars than on Earth. I was very slow at accomplishing tasks like getting dressed. I was always daydreaming. I liked it on Mars.

Most people regard the emotional atmosphere in the home as being of crucial importance in the development of the personality. It is usually considered to be a parental responsibility, though new studies of family life are taking into account interactions with other generations and the child's own behavior. Research into child-rearing has been fragmentary, and psychologists are only now beginning to understand the complex ways that these forces operate.

Parents are not smoothly functioning child-indoctrination machines, nor should they be. But they do have a number of powerful and persuasive means at their disposal to shape their children's behavior. Foremost among them is their power to reward and punish the child, based not only on the control of resources that the child considers to be desirable, but also on the child's emotional attachment to, and dependence on, the parent. Punishment may be effective as a means of eliminating or modifying unwanted responses, but the same punishment will have widely different effects on different children. Some psychological studies have shown that positive reinforcement is a more reliable, and therefore more predictable, means of changing behavior than is punishment. Nonetheless, many parents use corporal punishment when they believe that their children have misbehaved egregiously.

While the eccentric child's relations with his family are as profoundly formative as those of the normal child, there is no evidence that nonconformity can be implanted by child-rearing alone. Most eccentrics are raised by ordinary, conforming people, who are nearly always nonplussed by their child's deviant behavior. Conversely, the children of eccentrics may exhibit a compulsion to conform, to the dismay of their nonconformist parent.

The primary means of parental control over eccentric

children is hostile criticism. Few eccentrics look back upon their parents and siblings with warm, positive feelings. Their relationships with other family members were usually unhappy and tenuous; the father or the mother might equally have been the source of critical comments and arguments. Time and again, eccentrics in the study complained about extremely repressive and even abusive parents. Here are a few firsthand accounts of what it was like being on the receiving end of this sort of child-rearing:

> Very little emotion was expressed in my family except anger. My family thinks I am a deadbeat and always has. My parents were divorced in the early fifties, and they have been fighting World War III ever since. Megatons of criticism have been directed at me. When I was young, my father said, "I doubt he's even intelligent." So they gave me an IQ test. He then changed to, "We know you're intelligent, but . . ."

> I had no one to talk to in my teens. One felt simply like driftwood, and it never entered one's head to ask. It wasn't the done thing. I received every criticism under the sun.

> I remember once, when I was a little girl, I was second in the class and instead of praising me, my mother said, "Oh, second . . ." I always remember saying to her then, "And how would you feel if I had been twenty-second?" I think she was critical of me because she used to compare me with my father, whom she didn't like: "He tells lies and so do you." And I didn't really tell lies.

Of course, these comments present only one side. It must, after all, be tremendously stressful for a parent to have a child who, for example, gives baby sister a cigarette and abandons her on the street. A number of the eccentrics suggested themselves that they had precipitated their parents' anger and disappointment. Furthermore, the sense of having the world against them may have contributed to their evolving sense of originality and creativity.

These sensations of isolation and frustration at not being treated fairly become more acute for eccentric children when they enter school. Schools by their nature are systems that reward conformity and require the pupils to subordinate themselves to the teachers' pedagogy. Worse still, the young eccentric is frequently condescended to by the teacher. Eccentric children questioned not only educational methods and school procedures but also the content of their school work and sometimes its underlying philosophy. This comment came from an eccentric female professor whose IQ we measured at 150:

> I first realized I was odd when I went to school at the age of five. I thought the teachers were stupid. For instance, on my first day, they asked me if I would like a drink of milk. I said, "No, thank you." They insisted I drink it anyway. I thought how stupid the teacher was for asking me in the first place. I could already write my name, but she insisted that I keep a name card on my desk. This would have been all right if she had told me the reason was so that she could remember my name, or so that the other children would not feel in-

ferior, but I was not given a sensible reason. The teachers were always insisting that you go to the toilet when you didn't want to, that sort of thing. The reason I felt so odd is because other children seemed to accept that all this was quite normal, but I didn't.

Such feelings of superiority are common among young eccentrics, who as a result are rarely popular with their classmates. Those in our study said they escaped into books or fantasy worlds, and found these solitary interests more rewarding than group play, which seemed to them banal and pointless by comparison. This sensitivity to the banality and boredom of life continued into adulthood, and came to be something they took steps to avoid.

To the young eccentric, competition is merely a tedious frittering away of time, while cooperation means being held back by the less able. Given such attitudes, it is hardly surprising that other children regarded young eccentrics as nerds and oddballs: in most cases, they acted as if they were. We heard several childhood reminiscences resembling this one:

I found it very difficult to communicate with other children. I spent most of the breaks at school standing on my own in a corner of the playground. Whenever I tried to socialize with my fellow pupils, I was amazed by their pettiness, their selfishness, and most of all by their hypocrisy. I cried often, and children who are prone to crying are never popular at school. My four years at secondary school were probably the most miserable of my life. I had been bullied badly before, but now I was beaten up, kicked, spat on, and humiliated in a hundred other ways every single day. Because of this, I never went to college.

This tale, too, is one-sided. While we may sympathize with a child who cries a lot, it is not a sociable trait.

Occasionally, the young eccentric is a popular mischief-maker, a charismatic ringleader. One woman told us that she was bored in her early school years because she had already learned to read and write. In kindergarten, to amuse herself, she dared the other children to drink the ink out of a fountain pen. When they got sick, the teacher asked her mother to discipline her, but she couldn't, which caused the girl to disrespect both her mother and her teacher. Later, she recruited a gang of children, mostly boys, who sprayed passersby from her front yard with water pistols.

After she was expelled from school because of her disruptive influence, she was sent to a convent school. Within one term, her parents had been formally asked to remove her from there, as well. The list of offenses was an encyclopedia of naughtiness: she came to school barefoot, talked in class, ran in the corridors, failed to address the nuns properly, didn't stand up for the mother superior, and, worst of all, led her fellow pupils into open rebellion and sin. The latter charge, she explained, "simply meant that I asked them—incredulously—if they really believed in the Virgin Birth, and so forth. Punishment, even severe beatings, had no effect on me. I laughed in the face of it, and of course that made whoever was doing it even angrier."

The adolescent years explode with a white-hot intensity

169

that can startle parents, who often perceive it as gratuitous rebellion. It is such a common phenomenon that Anna Freud once went so far as to assert that adolescent rebellion is essential to becoming a well-adjusted adult. That was an exaggeration, if not a mistake. Recent research has shown that anywhere from 14 to 20 percent of adolescents never rebel at all, yet still go on to be normal adults. Anthropological fieldwork by Margaret Mead and others also indicates that adolescents in some societies do not rebel.

Many young eccentrics have already fought and won the battles of adolescence before their teen years arrive. Those who stood up to their families and teachers in childhood have a well-developed sense of their uniqueness, and pride in their independence. Their hard-won freedom outweighs the punishments they have received, and their courage has endowed them with the ability to stand up for unpopular causes. Eccentric teenagers can sometimes choose to be themselves with or without the approval of parents or peers.

An adolescent who has gained even a moderate degree of self-confidence and who goes his own way, unconcerned about whether or not he is popular, may find that his peers regard him as a tower of strength. During the first few years of adolescence there is increasing pressure to develop a coherent persona that comprehends both personal values and shifting group allegiances. The independent, eccentric adolescent accomplishes that earlier than average. In contrast, young eccentrics who are shy and withdrawn are neglected by their peers and emerge from adolescence socially isolated.

Early development of sexual characteristics and feelings is responsible for additional stress and rebellious behavior toward the parents. As the body image changes, adolescents experience a heightened concern about what the reactions of others to them will be. Those who undergo the physical changes at an earlier age tend to break more rules, more often. Early biological maturation may have long-term repercussions, particularly in regard to education and personal relationships. Here is a case in point from a young woman in the study:

At the age of eleven, I remember feeling sexy. I wore my new summer nightgown into the living room when we had a twelve-year-old boy and his mother visiting. I was promptly reprimanded by my mother, but pranced around in a halter top in front of the same boy a few weeks later. My parents got irate with me when I was chucked out of school for going out with choirboys. I went off and did all sorts of things that my parents did not approve of. My mama's ambition was for me to marry somebody rich, early. That would have been nice, but they were all so damn stupid I couldn't stand them. The biggest problem in my life has been men— men in the plural—and my total inability to say no. If a man wants to take me to bed, I say yes, because I am stupid.

Teenage eccentricity may be adaptive for a number of reasons. Such teenagers may prefer to be laughed at rather than ignored. By nonconforming, they are assured of some attention. Behavior that mocks convention and frustrates people in authority has great potential for fostering confidence about being oneself and knowledge of where one is going. A clear way to demonstrate this autonomy is to go against the grain, to antagonize, to oppose where there may be not very much external necessity to do so. This self-determining imperative results in affirmative action and an ineluctable independence of mind and thought. To possess that sort of autonomy is, in a very basic sense, to be free.

One of the most famous eccentric childhoods was that shared by the Mitford girls, which was immortalized by the eldest, Nancy, in her novels *The Pursuit of Love* and *Love in a Cold Climate,* and Jessica, the youngest, in her memoir *Hons and Rebels* (published as *Daughters and Rebels* in the United States). The six girls and their brother, Tom, were the children of Lord and Lady Redesdale, called by their children Farve and Muv.

Farve was a dashingly handsome man brimming over with vital spirits, a semiliterate aristocrat of limited means who lived for sport. Almost a child himself, Farve made life constantly interesting for the girls. The family kept a virtual menagerie, including mongooses, birds, snakes, toads and frogs, mice, chickens, a great many dogs, and a pony. Every few years Farve went to Canada to prospect for gold, always unsuccessfully.

He was openly hostile to books and book learning. Tom was sent to school because he was a boy; the girls, in Nancy Mitford's words, were "not educated" at home. When Farve served at the front in World War I, he wrote her a letter which read, in its entirety, "Dearest Koko, Many thanks for your last letter. Much love Farv." Lady Redesdale once tried to civilize her husband, and read *Tess of the D'Urbervilles* to him aloud. He was reduced to tears by Hardy's tragic tale, and his wife said to him, "Don't be so sad. It's only a novel." He roared back at her, "What! Not the *truth!* The damned feller invented all that?" He could never be persuaded to look at another book, until Nancy created a literary likeness of him in her novels. She later claimed that he was furious to learn that he didn't have a part in her biography of Madame de Pompadour.

Lady Redesdale was a placid, remote figure; according to Nancy, she "lived in a dream world of her own." She had some very peculiar notions about child-rearing, particularly with regard to health and diet. Although High Church to the core, she insisted that the girls observe the ancient Jewish dietary laws. When their brother, Tom, was sent to Eton, his first letter home stated simply: "We have sossages every day." His kosher sisters writhed in jealous agonies, but the "no pig" rule was never relaxed. Muv called the doctor only in cases of extreme illness, but any medicines he left were poured down the drain as soon as his back was turned.

Farve was a loving father but very changeable. At any given time, one of the girls was his favorite, and another was blamed for everything. The girls called the period of opprobrium Rat Week. Turns for Rat Week and being daddy's darling came suddenly and with no apparent cause, thus closely paralleling the childhood experiences of parental capriciousness reported by many of the eccentrics in our study.

The Mitford girls had a contrarian outlook from their earliest youth. When they were taken to see *Peter Pan* at the theater, at the point when Peter asked the children in the audience to say that they believed in fairies in order to save Tinker Bell's life, the Mitford girls loudly said, "No!" There was constant internecine warfare among them, with Nancy being the cruelest tormentor. In the opinion of her biographer, Selina Hastings, Nancy never recovered from the shock of dethronement when Pam, the second child, was born, and she devoted her childhood to making Pam's life miserable. She was just as remorseless in her persecution of the little ones. Tender-hearted Deborah was particularly susceptible. Nancy composed a sad poem about a poor little houseless match, which never failed to reduce Deborah to tears:

> A little houseless match
> It has no roof, no thatch
> If it's alone, it makes no moan
> That little houseless match.

Nancy was so adept at psychological torture that she could make Deborah cry at the dinner table simply by picking up a box of matches and showing it to her with a sad look.

In later life, however, it was the "victims," Pam and Deborah, who led the most tranquil and normal lives, marrying well and raising families. Deborah married the Duke of Devonshire, one of the richest men in England, becoming mistress of Chatsworth, one of its most magnificent houses. The fourth sister, Diana, left her husband for a married man, Sir Oswald Mosley, leader of the British Union of Fascists, and spent World War II languishing in prison for her support of fascism. Unity, the fifth child, went a step further and became a Nazi, a personal friend and possibly a lover of Adolf Hitler's. When Britain declared war, she had a breakdown and shot herself. Jessica, the youngest, went off in the opposite direction—anywhere but the center will do for eccentrics—and became an ardent Communist. She eloped with a cousin and ran away to Spain, where the civil war was raging. When World War II broke out, she moved to California, where she became an American citizen and a member of the Communist party. That made her, at least in Nancy's eyes, the most eccentric of all the Mitford girls.

EIGHT

The Eccentric Personality

Akenside was a young man warm with every notion connected with the sound of liberty, and by an eccentricity which such dispositions do not easily avoid, a lover of contradiction, and no friend to anything established.

—Samuel Johnson,
Lives of the English Poets: "Akenside"

WILLIAM JAMES ONCE REMARKED, "A MAN HAS AS MANY SOCIAL SELVES as there are people who recognize him." It is equally true that there are as many theories about the human personality as there are psychologists who have thought about the subject. However, since no theory has yet come up with a universal model for the normal personality, there is little reason to suppose that any of them would fit the eccentric personality. After all, not fitting is almost the definition of the eccentric: the square peg in the round hole.

The eccentric's way of interacting with the world can be

so fundamentally different that the standard psychological apparatus is almost useless in evaluating the eccentric personality. For example, one of the basic qualities that psychologists use to evaluate a person's personality is self-presentation. Five basic strategies of self-presentation have been described: ingratiation, intimidation, exemplification (being an example or model), supplication (relying on others for help), and self-promotion. Eccentrics do not pursue any of these strategies except the last, self-promotion, which occurs among them to a normal degree. Typically, eccentrics expend their mental energy on activities that do not require self-presentation, such as absorbing intellectual challenges. The whole category of self-presentation, as far as eccentrics are concerned, should be marked "does not apply." As it became increasingly clear to us that it was pointless to use theories of the personality based on the individual's ability to fit in to evaluate people who have no interest in fitting in, I developed some new, experimental criteria.

Since the perception of eccentricity is a subjective phenomenon, it seemed logical to look at it through the eyes of a normal person, as best as we could, and try to establish which qualities set a person apart as exceptional. Such an undertaking is, admittedly, simply putting an objective construction on the subjective, but that is the essence of psychology. It was the first time that a psychologist had examined what constitutes an exceptional personality.

I formulated five basic perceived qualities of the exceptional person, which we then put to the test by comparing the eccentrics in our sample against established norms. I doubt whether these criteria are comprehensive, or that any set ever could be; for exceptionality, as a concept and as a way of seeing human nature, is an elusive essence. We all recognize, or rather we think we recognize, exceptions with confidence, but these judgments are often based on partial knowledge or even intuition.

The five criteria of exceptionality were rarity, extremity, the possession of special attributes, the possession of unusual combinations of attributes, and doing ordinary things in extraordinary ways.

Rarity

It might seem obvious to state that rarity is an attribute of exceptionality—the two are dictionary synonyms—but we were curious to put a number on eccentricity. After all, it has to be rare enough to be . . . well, exceptional, yet it is nonetheless something that we have all encountered. Based on standard statistical analysis, as we have stated, we found the prevalence of classic eccentrics in the general population to be approximately 1 in 10,000, with a margin of error that might be as high as plus or minus 50 percent.

In addition, there may be many more people who share some but not all of the qualities of the dyed-in-the-wool eccentric. Eccentricity is much more than a chance mutation or a fluke of human nature: it is an innate human propensity that is present to a varying degree in everyone. Probably many more people have the potential and predisposition to be eccentric than ever have the opportunity, effrontery, and bravery to do so. This second, more frequent variant could be as much as a hundred times more numerous, possibly amounting to more than two million Americans and half a million people in Britain.

Extremity

Most people are near the average on most dimensions of normal personality: that's why it's called the average. Moreover, when they are given standardized personality tests, very few people manifest extremely high or extremely low scores on any given trait. While it is true that such tests are nearly useless for evaluating the eccentric personality, we decided that it might nonetheless be a good idea to administer one experimentally to the sample, to generate some raw data about the extent to which eccentrics exceed the norms established for the rest of us. The test we chose was the 16PF, the best-validated personality test now in use throughout the world. Designed by the American psychologist Raymond Cattell, it consists of 187 statements, each offering three possible answers. It embraces all the major factors of the personality, which in Cattell's system number sixteen.

Results on the 16PF are measured on a ten-point scale, where 1 represents virtual absence of the trait and 10 the saturation point. Such extremely low or extremely high levels of any dimension of personality are shown by only 2.3 percent of those taking the test. Psychologists have long considered such extreme personality traits to be quite rare. Although strong mathematical principles have been marshaled in support of this supposition, no empirical evidence had ever been presented for or against it. Such an analysis was long overdue, if for no other reason than for assurance that certain bedrock concepts of statistics, such as normal distribution curves and probabilities, apply to the intangibles of human nature.

The smooth continuity of the bulging middle of the graph ought not to rule out wild diversity at the extremes. In the natural sciences, it is well known that funny things happen at the extremes—thus high-energy particle physics, low-temperature physics, zero-gravity effects, and so forth. Why shouldn't this tendency to bizarre and exotic effects at the extremes apply equally to the workings of the human mind?

As you will see from the table opposite, the eccentrics handily overtopped, many times over, the 2.3 percent threshold for extreme values. Remember, these figures only reflect those at the very extreme ends of the spectrum; subjects scoring a 2 or a 9 in any of these traits, which we would still call somewhat extreme, are not included. Nearly every personality trait on the 16PF test was present in some of the eccentrics to an extreme degree, whether positively or negatively. The results for assertiveness were especially high, but not surprising, for being a full-time eccentric requires an extraordinary amount of courage and self-confidence.

Special Attributes

In addition to the extremes of personality measured clinically by the 16PF test, eccentrics also tend to exhibit extremism in their pursuits in life. They do nothing by half measures, exhibiting a boundless enthusiasm that can lead them to take on special attributes that set them apart as exceptional.

Eccentric Subjects with Extreme Personality Traits (%)

16PF Personality Factor	Males	Females
Dominant, assertive	14	39
Intelligent, bright	15	15
Forthright, unpretentious	15	14
Suspicious	11	10
Imaginative, bohemian	11	8
Bold, venturesome	7	11
Reserved, detached	5	5
Self-assured, placid	3	10
Self-sufficient, resourceful	10	7
Radical	5	6
Tough-minded, hard	4	5
Follows own urges	1	8
Relaxed, tranquil	4	6
Expedient, disregards rules	6	6
Shy, timid	7	1
Affected by feelings	7	3
Serious	3	5
Impulsive	6	2
Emotionally stable	5	4
Tender-minded, sensitive	6	3

Often, this comes about as the result of the eccentric's curiosity, which knows no limits. If, for instance, an ordinary person wanted to know about electricity, he would most likely read a book on the subject, or perhaps watch a television documentary. An eccentric would read much more, and to a greater depth. He might also call the local electrical authority and arrange to observe a power generator in operation, to see how it works. Then he might knock on the door of a physics or engineering professor to ask questions, which would seem alternately naive and learned.

Such total immersion in a subject, sometimes to the exclusion of all else, can lead a person to identify closely with the subject and the personalities involved in it, a state of empathy approaching obsession. Several of the British eccentrics in the study were absorbed by the legend of Robin Hood. One man identified himself so deeply with the hero who stole from the rich and gave to the poor that he moved to Sherwood Forest and legally adopted the name. He now wears a historically accurate medieval forester's costume— all in green, complete with longbow, a quiverful of arrows, and a feathered hat—seven days a week. Ironically, before he became Robin Hood, he earned his living by installing automatic teller machines and bank security equipment.

We also encountered a feminist Robina, a woman with strong views who used the Robin Hood image to make a point. Otherwise a successful academic, she is more interested in cross-dressing than in the redistribution of wealth: Robina enjoys the effect she creates when she dons her green costume and strides purposefully around town. Another pretender, whose real name is Robin St. Claire, shares a trailer home on the shores of Lake Windermere, in Cumbria, with his girlfriend, Maid Marian. The two of them are seen in full regalia drinking with the merry men and maids at pubs in the Lake District.

Less ostentatious is John Goodheart, who usually forgoes

the dressing up but insists that he is related to the historical figure upon whom the Robin Hood legends are based, Robin Fitzodo de Locksley. After years of patient heraldic investigations at the British Museum, Goodheart, a highly respected civil servant, hopes to take his case to the European Court of Human Rights to claim the title Lord John Pope-de-Locksley, K.O.T.O. (We never did find out what those initials stood for.)

It is important to draw a distinction here between a person experiencing delusional mania—the popular image of the raving lunatic who thinks he's Napoleon—and the eccentric. These people know that they're not really Robin Hood; they're able to look around themselves and see that they don't live in a medieval romance. Rather, they have taken their vivid imaginings a step further: instead of idly daydreaming about how delightful it would be to escape their dreary, workaday world and lead the romantic life of Robin Hood, they do it. It may only be make-believe, but their fecund, powerful imaginations permit them to take belief to a higher level.

Other eccentrics, instead of identifying with a person, become obsessed with a thing. Alan Fairweather's overriding interest in life is the potato—its history, how to clone it, how to grow it, every possible aspect of the vegetable. Fairweather is thus superbly qualified for his position as a potato inspector for the Ministry of Agriculture, Fisheries and Food in Scotland, a job he carries out, obviously, with great enthusiasm. Every meal he eats consists entirely of potatoes, two pounds of them, topped off with a chocolate bar, the occasional vitamin pill, and many pots of tea.

"Potatoes provide all the nourishment I need," he says. "I can't be bothered to cook anything else." He needs little encouragement to expound on the socio-political repercussions of the tuber, or the best ways to cook its hundred or so varieties. (His favorite recipe: plunge without peeling into boiling salted water; after twenty minutes juggle them around in a hot, dry skillet to make them fluffy.) Fairweather spends his holidays every year in South America, where he believes the potato evolved. He sleeps on the floor of his study in a sleeping bag and rents out all four of the bedrooms in his house: "I don't see the point in having a special room set aside to fall unconscious in."

Most eccentrics possess an extraordinary, but typically erratic, sense of humor. However, it can sometimes lead them into making lapses from good taste when they have pointed comments to make about social conventions. For example, an Oxford-educated Jamaican with a surreal philosophy about life would turn up for job interviews dressed in top hat, white tie, and tails. He explained this by saying, "The way to avoid being flushed down the toilet is never to conform to straight society's values." He said that a friend of his told him, "If everyone carried on like you, the world would go to the dogs." To this he replied, "It's the squares who traffic in wars who are sending the world to the dogs."

Eccentrics can be extreme in the exuberance with which they express their sense of humor; the way normal people regard the eccentric often depends upon what they find funny. Not everyone is amused by the antics of one eccentric, whose penchant for practical jokes is described here by a friend:

ECCENTRICS

He collects suits of armor and Indian knickknacks, lives in a large Georgian mansion, and has some strange habits. His mildest kind of practical joke is to push a dish of meringue trifle into the face of a lady guest at a smart dinner party in his home, having first asked her to smell it to see if it is "off." There is an oubliette under one of his dining room chairs, and any boring guest is seated over it and dropped into the wine cellar when he can stand no more. His *coup de grâce* was the miniature bomb that he planted inside his son's birthday cake, which the boy detonated by blowing on the candles, covering all his little friends with icing. The man's long-suffering wife had to clean them all up, then explain and apologize to their parents after the party.

Eccentric humor is broad in scope, embracing the gentle as well as the explosive. Auntie Barbara Hovanetz, of Winter Park, Florida, is the president and founding mother of the National Frumps of America. A frump, according to Hovanetz, is a Frugal, Responsible, Unpretentious, Mature Person. "We carry library cards and a wallet full of pictures of our kids and our dog," she explained. "We eat bologna on white bread and look for bargains in the 'scratch and dent' section of the supermarket." It all started with her circle of friends at the University of Iowa. "My friends and I were too nice to be rebels. We bowled and played miniature golf and grew African violets in empty margarine containers in our dorm rooms."

Hovanetz and her friends never lost their frumpish ways, and at their twentieth class reunion, over the meatloaf special at Howard Johnson's, they founded the NFA. She says that what attracted her to her husband, Uncle Ed, wasn't his money and good looks but rather "his collection of mismatched shoelaces and dried-up ballpoint pens." Hovanetz obviously has her tongue planted firmly in her cheek, but there is nonetheless a streak of earnestness running through her devotion to the frump cause: a normal person might jokingly call herself a frump, but going to the extreme of establishing a society that issues membership cards and publishes a newsletter sets her apart as exceptional.

The funniest eccentrics are those who do things with a straight face, blithely unaware that people are laughing at them, such as the well-heeled lady described in this extract:

My mother could always be relied on to do the unexpected. Her real forte was staircases. She ripped them out and rerouted them with gay abandon. She waltzed the good one around the house for five years—never, of course, having it fixed. The only way to the second and third floors was by outside ladder. In my sixties, I can still shinny up a ladder three stories high. She chopped the house in half before the staircase finally came down, and she took it with her when she sold the house. I don't think I ever could persuade removal men to take a concert grand piano up a spiral staircase, but she persuaded them it could be done—and after each abortive attempt she plied them with expensive single-malt whisky. When they all accepted defeat we had three tight movers and a piano minus its legs, lid, and pedals.

Then the fun really started. She wanted to call the builder to reroute the staircase again. How he did it I don't know, but by nine o'clock the next morning my father had procured a carpenter and a mobile crane. The window was taken out and the piano installed. Why she carted that piano around was like everything else: never explained. One thing was certain, she never learned to play it.

Unusual Combinations of Behaviors and Attributes

Eccentrics of the past appear, at first glance, to be better at this than their modern counterparts. About half of the historical sample appear to have been eccentric in two or more different ways. Gerald Tyrwhitt-Wilson, fourteenth Baron Berners (1883–1950), indulged every whim that swam into his brain. Aside from being a talented composer whose ballets were staged by Diaghilev and Ashton, and a novelist of distinction, he dyed his pet doves every color of the rainbow, wrote scatological verse, and once had a horse as a guest at a formal tea party in the parlor of his ancestral home, Faringdon House, in Berkshire. He built a folly in his garden there, a 140-foot-high tower with a sign reading "Members of the public committing suicide from this tower do so at their own risk." (He was a neighbor of the Mitfords; Nancy Mitford closely modeled Lord Merlin in *The Pursuit of Love* on him.)

Like many eccentrics, Lord Berners was a collector and an accomplished practical joker. Among other things, he collected people's calling cards. Once when he had lent his villa in Rome to a pair of honeymooners, he sent ahead to the butler a packet of the calling cards of society's most celebrated bores, none of whom was anywhere near Rome. Whenever the young couple went out, the servant placed a few of the cards in the salver for them to find when they returned. One of Lord Berners' friends, the composer Constant Lambert, described how he kept strangers out of his railway compartment: "Donning black spectacles, he would, with a look of fiendish expectation, beckon in the passersby. Those isolated figures who took the risk became so perturbed by his habit of reading the papers upside-down and taking his temperature every five minutes that they invariably got out at the next station."

Lord Berner's epitaph, which he wrote himself, could stand as a eulogy for many eccentrics:

> Here lies Lord Berners,
> One of the learners.
> His great love of learning
> May earn him a burning.
>
> But praise to the Lord,
> He was never bored!

Those who did not manifest their eccentricity in several different ways were motivated by one single-minded purpose, whether frugality, finding solitude, or being universally kind, which they carried to bizarre extremes. Inadvertently, along the way they attracted attention for their exceptional behavior. For instance, all that Thomas Birch, a librarian in London in the eighteenth century, wanted to do was to emulate Izaak Walton and become the compleat angler. His ambition led him to disguise himself as a tree, in a costume cleverly designed to make his arms look like branches and the fishing line a floating blossom. History does not tell us how successful he was at catching fish, but it does record that he frightened the daylights out of people walking by when he spoke or moved.

Modern eccentrics concentrate their efforts on even more diverse repertoires of outrageous behaviors. Some of our subjects found ways to innovate at work while amazing their friends and acquaintances with their exceptional behavior and dazzling disregard of what anyone might think. John Slater is such a man. Currently living in one of the most remote parts of the Western Highlands, he is the only person ever to have walked from Land's End to John O'Groats in his bare feet, wearing only his striped pajamas and accompanied by his pet labrador, Guinness. The dog, unlike his master, was shod, with two pairs of suede booties.

Slater's occupational career has been a checkered one: Royal Marine bandsman, Commando, truck driver, steward on a luxury yacht, social worker with the mentally handicapped, salesman, insurance broker, waiter, driftwood artist, painter and decorator, public speaker, and fund-raiser. He once volunteered to spend six months in a cage in London Zoo as a human exhibit, to help raise funds for the conservation of the panda. The zoo authorities, he said, "foolishly declined." At that time he lived with down-and-outs in London, so that he could help others and learn more about himself. When he got home he appointed a 250-pound sheepdog named Tiny to a directorship of his tour-guide company.

For most of the past ten years, Slater has lived in a cave, which is flooded with seawater at high tide. He explains:

There is a cathedral-like silence in caves which helps me to think and work things out. I'm addicted to harmony, peace of mind, restfulness. There's so much spending on the quality of death and nothing on the quality of life. I'm nursing all this terrific idealism, always thinking about what I can do next. I gave a friend of mine a brand name for his new wholemeal bakery—Thoroughbread. And why hasn't someone marketed a unisex deodorant called "Every Body"?

On the occasion of Slater's third marriage, his new wife insisted that he desist from cave-dwelling and live with her in a modern stone cottage. He made a valiant effort to reform, but like Huckleberry Finn he kept slipping away. Finally his wife gave him an ultimatum, in effect, "It's me or the cave." He finally left her and went back to the cave. Slater's life goal, he says, is to raise a million pounds for charity. His motto is "Wag your tail at everyone you meet."

Some eccentrics quietly invent a satisfying niche compatible with their intellectual needs, and remain in it peacefully and brilliantly, preoccupied for long periods. Helga Schiller follows this pattern. From her early childhood in Germany, she was told that she was special and unusual. She was an only child until she was twelve years old. "One was always made to feel wanted and loved and cherished and treasured," she said. Her mother remarried when she was thirteen, and her stepfather attempted, unsuccessfully, first to cajole and then to coerce her into having sex with him. Because of her intellectual and athletic abilities, she was invited to join the Nazi party, but she refused on moral and ethical grounds. "How could anyone presume to control me?" she exclaimed indignantly. "My teachers tried, my husband tried, the state tried. I'm the only one who controls me."

Schiller later obtained degrees in languages and education from the universities of Cologne, Dundee, London, and Edinburgh. She studies all day long, every day, and has a measured IQ of over 165. She told us:

> If I know the truth, I can cope with it. I would be full of brilliant ideas . . . then people would befriend me and then pinch my thoughts. Mentally I'm firing on all my 2,559 cylinders. Twenty-four hours isn't enough for living—now if I were twins! Or quadruplets! Or if I could clone myself, what fun I would have!

About half the women and three-quarters of the men in the study possessed a number of special talents and attributes, and expressed their eccentricities in a variety of ways. Slightly more than a third of them also felt that they contained within themselves at least one other personality that was different from themselves. This other personality ought not to be confused with schizophrenia or multiple personality, in the mold of *The Three Faces of Eve* or *Sybil;* it is probably closer to a secret wish. The women most often described the other self as uninhibited, sexy, and successful. For the men, the preferred alter ego was described as self-confident, adventurous, and successful. It may have been the eccentrics' way of saying that they wished they were even more extrovert and outgoing. In addition, the women subjects may have been expressing an urge to be less hampered by the dictates of convention and conscience.

Doing Ordinary Things in Extraordinary Ways

Since the time of the Roman Republic, at least, employers have thought it their duty to teach their workers and servants, but a British farmer named John Alington (1795–1863) took this notion to an eccentric extreme. He transformed a pond on his farm into a scale model of the world, and while his workers rowed him around the different countries in his microcosm, he lectured them on geography. Before taking them to London for the Great Exhibition of 1851, Alington required them to construct a large log model of the streets of London between Hyde Park and King's Cross. This project proved to be such a disaster that Alington declared that his men were too stupid to be trusted not to get lost, and so he canceled the trip.

Francis Waring (1760–1833), the vicar of Heybridge in Essex, performed all the duties of his office, but in an extraordinary way. He read his church lessons at breakneck speed, gave a very brief sermon, not much longer than a quick-fire aphorism or two, ran down the aisle, leaped onto a fast horse, and rode at a gallop to repeat this effort at two other churches. His everyday domestic arrangements were also peculiar. Though not poor, he furnished his vicarage with rough-hewn logs rather than chairs; his children ate their meals from a trough beside the split-log dining table; and he and his wife slept in an enormous wicker cradle suspended from the ceiling.

Doing ordinary things in extraordinary ways has always been a trait of the eccentric. The modern counterparts of Alington and Waring still behave in this way: they can be relied on to find alternative means to do things that others usually accept without a second thought. Sometimes, this involves unusual eating and sleeping arrangements, housing, ways of writing, transport, the conduct of interpersonal relationships—indeed the whole gamut of human activities.

Such behavior often occurs in the context of a deliberately altered lifestyle. David McDermott, the time-tripping artist in New York, says that he reads only books published before the twentieth century. "I like to read the double-deckers. Sometimes I read the second volume first, then the first one. If one of the volumes is missing, that doesn't bother me. We only had volume two of a three-volume set of *Robinson Crusoe,* so I just read that one."

Andy Bruce-Wallace decided at the age of twenty-four that he would escape city life. He now lives in the bombed-out shell of a house in Northern Ireland, whose previous occupant had been a police officer in the Royal Ulster Constabulary who was killed by the IRA. Bruce-Wallace grows all the food he needs in a large organic garden. He travels everywhere on a tall, odd-looking tricycle of his own design, packing all his camping and cooking facilities with him: "Distance no object," he says. He is a recluse by choice, and an environmentalist who follows some teachings of Taoism.

Bruce-Wallace's eccentricity first manifested itself when he was a thirteen-year-old boy growing up in the Lake

District and the Yorkshire dales. He converted the family garage into a room of his own, then shut himself off from his family and everyone else, even refusing to be photographed. He walked to school barefoot in order to harden himself. Then he moved out of the house altogether, to a tent in his family's garden. By stages he progressed to the point where he stayed out-of-doors most of the time, pitting himself against the elements on the mountains of northern England and the Scottish Highlands. He walked very long distances, and slept in the open if it was foggy. In Ireland, he has come to be known by his friends as "the Yeti." In addition to tending his crops and herbs, Bruce-Wallace also writes tongue-in-cheek letters to newspapers under assumed names, such as P. Kropotkan and Gerald Winstanley.

A number of eccentrics in the sample showed the first overt indications of their eccentricity by being against some fixture of modern life; several of them, for instance, were vehemently anti-automobile. Twenty of the subjects were opposed to the tenets and practices of modern medicine. Ten of them have acted on these beliefs to the point of practicing alternative medicine themselves.

Eccentrics can also become active moralizers and proselytizers. Stanley Green, the most famous sandwich-board man in the West End of London, was one of these. He was deeply affected by a Sunday school teacher who told the class, "Don't listen to dirty jokes. Walk away from them." Green went on to become moral to an extreme: "I've spoiled my life by being too honest. I refused to do dishonest things when expected to do so on two occasions, and lost good jobs that way." He worked in the Civil Service and local government, but decided at the age of fifty-three to devote himself to publicizing his theory that "less protein means less lust."

About a quarter of the eccentrics in the study fulfilled all these criteria for exceptionality. The great majority of the subjects manifested at least two of the criteria, and many of them more than three.

The overriding conclusion to be drawn from this analysis is that being exceptional is far from a disadvantage. Indeed, it can be a positive attribute. Inconsistencies and contradictions in personality reflect one or more possible states of a person's nature. Our potential selves are suspended in a realm of total possibility. To become a self-invented person is to exercise a unique prerogative of life; it is brilliant egomania to say that you belong to yourself. Selfhood depends on the assertion of identity, whether it be done to defy the forces of power, of control, or even those of tedium. To this end, it almost becomes a necessity to pit oneself against order and uniformity in order to expand the borders of personality. An eccentric does this, however much his social environment may be indifferent or hostile to such an experiment in subjectivity.

The enhancement of selfhood sometimes means that one may not go along with the crowd, nor placidly accept being integrated into a world of prescribed social definitions. This choice can leave the eccentric in a situation fraught with ambiguity: the only significant limitation to a person's inter-pretation of his actions, in the end, is that created by social conventions. To burst these constraints and break down these barriers is a creative act itself, and it may open wide the floodgates of creativity for the individual who is brave enough to do so.

NINE

The Psycholinguistic Analysis

"But 'glory' doesn't mean 'a nice knock-down argument,' "
Alice objected.

"When I use a word," Humpty Dumpty said, in a rather
scornful tone, "it means just what I choose it to mean—
neither more nor less."

"The question is," said Alice, "whether you can make
words mean so many different things."

"The question is," said Humpty Dumpty, "which is to be
master—that's all."

—*Lewis Carroll,*
Through the Looking Glass

THERE IS NO WAY TO ASK AN ECCENTRIC TO EXPLAIN WHY HE IS THE
way he is. It isn't like asking people why they are happy or
unhappy, because normal, healthy people usually have
good reasons for their emotional states: we're happy when
we get a pay raise, unhappy when our car breaks down.

A closer analogy would be asking smart people why they are smart, or creative people why they are creative. Either they will truthfully say they have no idea—"That's just the way I am"—or they will respond with verbal formulations that are themselves instances of the qualities in question. The smart person might explain to you all the latest research into human intelligence, talking knowledgeably about synapses and neurotransmitters, thereby demonstrating his ability to comprehend scientific studies—an instance of his intelligence. The creative person might reply to the question with a striking image or a story—an instance of his creativity. Yet it is impossible for anyone to comment objectively about his own mental processes, since the only way to do so is by using those very processes. As you would expect, when eccentrics are asked to comment on their eccentricity, their responses tend to be eccentric.

Aldous Huxley once estimated, I know not how, that 70 percent of human existence is dominated by language and verbal thought. The one intellectual ability that all the eccentrics in our study had in common was fluency in English, so language presented itself as one possible medium through which to objectify some of the subjective issues surrounding eccentricity. Then we hit upon the idea of applying standard psycholinguistic analysis to the taped speech samples we had made when we interviewed the subjects. In 1986 a new method for the assessment of thought, language, and communication (TLC) was published by a psychiatrist named Nancy Andreasen, a professor at the University of Iowa. The TLC scale was originally designed as an aid in diagnosing and measuring schizophrenia; therefore, given the results we obtained from the Present State Examination, showing that serious schizophrenic symptoms were actually less common among eccentrics than the general population, we were very cautious about using the TLC as a tool for studying eccentrics.

It is an open secret in psychology that schizophrenia is an idea without an essence, an artificial diagnostic category whose boundaries do not conform to what is there in nature. While it is true that there are people who become severely disturbed in what they perceive, think, and do, science remains profoundly uncertain as to the causes and even the pathology of their illness or illnesses. Thus it verges on intellectual hubris to apply objective psycholinguistics to such a group, and applying it to an entirely different phenomenon such as eccentricity might seem to be a scientific shot in the dark.

To a certain extent it was. But we decided that eccentrics might make a good comparison group, for while they exhibit some of the thought and language characteristics of schizophrenics, they are more readily comprehensible: for all their battiness, eccentrics are not insane, and however unorthodox their individual adaptations, they are usually functioning members of society. Schizophrenics are not ordinarily aware of the inconsistencies in their use of language, but eccentrics are—either they just don't care or they actually cultivate their linguistic peculiarities. And there was the tantalizing possibility that psycholinguistic analysis might yield some fresh insights into the nature of eccentricity.

The TLC scale is a collaboration between linguistic experts and psychiatrists, using specialized computer programs to analyze spoken language. It defines twenty distinct thought, language, and communication disorders, which can be identified and measured against a carefully defined norm; five of these seem to pertain only to schizophrenics, so we need not address them here. Most of the time, language behavior involves a face-to-face interaction between a speaker and a listener. Disorders occur because the speaker fails to follow the formal and informal rules that enable people to understand one another. When the speaker fails to take the needs of the listener into account, the result is usually a mild communication disorder. Language disorders, the second main type, are those in which the speaker violates the normal syntactical and semantic conventions that govern language usage. Thought disorders, the most fundamental, result from an inability to think clearly enough to communicate correctly. These are the fifteen disorders we looked for in the speech samples of the eccentrics:

- poverty of speech, having little or nothing to say on any subject;
- poverty of content of speech, language that is vague and repetitive, saying very little in many words;
- pressure of speech, or accelerated tempo;
- distractible speech, changing the subject abruptly;
- tangentiality, replying to a question in an oblique or irrelevant manner;
- derailment, slipping from one train of thought to another

one that is obliquely related, or even completely unrelated;

- illogicality;
- clanging, a pattern of speech in which sound rather than meaning governs word choices;
- word approximations, using ordinary words in new and unconventional ways, or coining new words and phrases (e.g., calling a pen a "paperskate," or a watch a "time vessel");
- circumstantiality, speech that is minutely and unnecessarily detailed, or excessively circuitous in reaching its goal;
- loss of goal, failure to follow a chain of thought through to its natural conclusion;
- perseveration, persistent repetition of words or ideas, sometimes out of context;
- blocking, interruption of a train of speech before the thought has been completed;
- stilted speech; and
- self-reference, bringing in the subject of oneself obsessively or in inappropriate ways.

We systematically evaluated each of the ninety-minute audio tapes we had obtained using this scale. It is impossible to be exact about something like poverty of speech; a lot of what one hears on radio and television today would seem to many of us to be impoverished of speech. However, we made our judgments by comparing the extracts from the eccentric subjects against the whole range of normal human speech, as objectively as we were able. In other words, we were using the broadest standard, the lowest common denominator, and not making any value judgments about the intellectual quality of our subjects' utterances.

This verbatim excerpt, from a sixty-six-year-old British eccentric named Brendan who has developed some highly arcane theories about human nature, exhibits at least seven different types of linguistic disorder (the ellipses indicate pauses):

> I have since resolved to actually Sherlock Holmes a manuscript, anticipatory, of many practicing psychiatry, this conjectural profession, none to date have concentrated their probes into the mind's cognitive faculties, which . . . I suspect . . . is . . . as it were, a high-octane, rather than the typically average petrol . . . that circumstances, IQ and health, is responsible for neurosis. Is it a key to the wonderful fulfillment of this gift of life? Whiter light needs darker shadow. The grayest gap in psychiatry is that it must accept creative individuals are left to stew in their own portentous juices to work out their eccentricity unaided.
>
> Your trained mind could tolerate my ineffectuality of knowledge. . . . You may gladly have the bones of my lifetime journey. . . . Biology made me an ineffectual creature-spirit, brooding over chaos. I longed to be an artist. My sensitivity turned into one-hundred-percent pacifism, befitting my physical unmanliness, deemed cowardice. So be it. . . . I did not make myself. . . . My errors may have compounded my naiveté lack of worldly wise. To add fear to fearfulness is cruelty. Thought has been a permanent friend

. . . and enemy . . . to try and reason with lifelong regret of ignorance of life and how it is lived. Why is the one word always with me. Inflationally richer in ersatz money, and to have learned what little impact the born introverted mind has on society, the eccentric can be consoled of their bijou part through life, which the gregarious have made less secure than the simplicity of my childhood. No earth could be more wonderful, no altruism, so trampled by the sheer forces opposing peace . . . and harmony . . . which the populist mind chooses as its rights. Why I even got into the pod of civilization's green peas, ancestry alone knows.

At a subjective level, there is some poignant poetry in Brendan's heartfelt outpouring, but at several points the associative threads became unraveled (derailment). The tempo of his speech on the tape was speeded up (pressure of speech). The second paragraph exhibited a moderately abnormal degree of self-reference. Stilted speech was evident in the use of a quaint Victorianism such as "bijou," and using "Sherlock Holmes" as a verb is an instance of word approximation. Several unfinished clauses ran into new ones without full logical connections between them (illogicality). There was even a single occurrence, albeit a fairly tenuous one, of clanging in the last two sentences ("peace" and "peas").

This passage demonstrates how several mild to moderate linguistic abnormalities can combine to give a distinctly odd ring to a person's speech. Outside the artificial situation of a research interview, normal people might lose patience with such a speaker, even to the point of ridiculing him. As some of our subjects themselves have noted, there is not much room these days for extremely original or flowery speech.

After we had analyzed the taped samples, we compared the results with the values for normal subjects that had been used as the control by the scale's originator. It turned out to be quite an intriguing comparison. This table opposite sets the frequency of thought, language, and communication disorders in the speech of eccentrics alongside those of normal people.

Not too much ought to be made of this: 64 percent of female eccentrics and 48 percent of male eccentrics had no language abnormalities of any kind, and even when the eccentric's way of speaking was extremely convoluted, we could almost always follow what he was saying. Yet the points where the eccentrics departed markedly from the norm proved to be uncommonly instructive. The two disorders that are much *less* frequent among eccentrics than normal people—derailment and loss of goal—reflect the eccentric's propensity for obsession. A normal person's attention is much more likely to be distracted, but an eccentric will maunder on relentlessly, regardless of fire or flood, and if his interlocutor walks out of the room, he will follow him.

There is a glaring paradox in describing as disorders patterns of speech more frequent among normal people, the control group, than among eccentric people. It might make more sense to phrase it positively, to say that eccentrics are mildly deficient in normal digressiveness, a trait possessing

Frequency of Thought, Language, and Communication Abnormalities (%)

	Normal People	Eccentric People
Poverty of speech	5	10
Poverty of content of speech	1	0
Pressure of speech	6	35
Distractible speech	3	0
Tangentiality	2	33
Derailment	32	4
Illogicality	0	4
Clanging	0	1
Word approximations	2	0
Circumstantiality	6	32
Loss of goal	18	6
Perseveration	8	2
Blocking	1	2
Stilted speech	1	2
Self-reference	1	28

positive, cooperative social value. The Belgian linguist Patricia Niedzwieki, working at the Sorbonne, has accumulated persuasive experimental evidence favoring this hypothesis. She has linked digressiveness to sex differences (men digress less), emotional responsiveness, and constructive nonlinear thinking. Judith Hall at the Johns Hopkins University, in reviewing 125 previous psychological studies, has also provided evidence that lends weight to this idea. If these assumptions are correct, some eccentrics may be deficient in normal digressiveness.

Two other significant deviations in eccentric speech are the higher levels of tangentiality and circumstantiality. These terms sound like polysyllabic scholarese for the same thing, and to a certain extent they are. The difference is that tangentiality refers to a seemingly irrelevant answer to the interviewer's question, while circumstantiality is used to describe circuitous speech patterns—beating around the bush. On the face of it, it might seem that the eccentrics' tendency toward tangentiality and circumstantiality conflicts with their low measured levels of digressiveness. Yet this apparent paradox actually provides a neat description of many eccentrics: while they may be bizarre and elliptical in the way they reach their goals, they are dogged about finally reaching them, however long and strange the ride. There is a method in their madness.

Here are two verbatim extracts from our interviews with eccentrics in the study, which illustrate these qualities. The first is from Felix, a forty-year-old man from London:

> I had my Alaskan husky puppy's skin tanned and the pelt hangs on my front veranda. . . . I've asked that my own carcass is to be freeze-dried and mounted over the fireplace . . . coming from the philosophy of each of us being the center of our own universe and *everything* that we are I am conscious of, I am responsible for. There are no accidents. There is no blame. There is only choice.

Moving circuitously from the specific to the general, he finally arrives at his conceptual goal, a remarkably expansive and ebullient view of his place in the universe.

The second example comes from Leo Shelley, a poet from Edinburgh who reads his own and other poets' works in an informal broadcast over citizens band radio. A modern-day Oscar Wilde, he believes it is his mission to bring beauty and "felicity of thought," as he puts it, to the lives of ordinary people, especially truckers, the unemployed, and the disabled.

Interviewer: Are you a collector?

Shelley: Yes. I do . . . the collection comes down to this. . . . If someone says to me I have a rhyme for your CB broadcast . . . my first answer would be . . . did you? . . . or the question would be . . . did you do it yourself? Now I am interested if he or she did it themselves. . . . It doesn't matter what it sounds like, what is of interest to me is what it sounds like, but it is more important that they did it themselves. If it is something, say Wordsworth . . . then I am sorry, I am not interested. I am only interested in the immediate . . . what you or yours experience. If I want Wordsworth then I suppose I would go and get him and explain it to myself one way or another, but I don't want that, but I do want this one. That is the difference . . . I collect that . . . I don't collect Wordsworth, but I do collect the aspiring or the clever.

I will take anything—virtually the most prosaic thing, and I can kick it into a story, for instance, verses really to me are little stories, it just so happens that I put them into verse, maybe one verse. If so then these are the most difficult, because you have to get a beginning, a middle, and an end, all in one verse—if you have got more—I take any subject like that.

Both these extracts were delivered at an aberrantly rapid tempo—the quality called pressure of speech on the TLC scale, the single speech disorder most commonly observed in eccentrics. The driven quality of eccentrics' speech and their penchant for circumstantiality are components of a phenomenon psychologists call "fluent disorganization," which is used to describe the characteristic long-windedness of eccentrics. Mark Twain recognized fluent disorganization: after hearing a revolutionary fanatic who had been inciting Americans to invade Canada, he remarked, "This person could be made really useful by roosting him on some lighthouse or other prominence where storms prevail, because it takes so much wind to keep him going that he probably moves in the midst of a dead calm wherever he travels!"

Another extreme divergence from the norm was the high proportion of eccentrics who showed abnormal self-reference, where the speaker repeatedly turns the conversation back to himself, even when the subject under discussion has no apparent connection with him. This feature of eccentric speech cannot be properly evaluated on the basis of a psychodiagnostic interview, since the whole point of the interview is to get the subject to talk about himself. However, self-reference may be observed validly during informal conversations about neutral topics, and many of our questions allowed for that.

Even more peculiar, several eccentrics in the study, while highly self-referencing, consistently referred to themselves in the third person. We found that for male eccentrics, but not female eccentrics, there was a significant inverse relationship between self-reference and intelligence; in other words, the more intelligent male eccentrics tended to be less self-referencing, and vice versa. Yet strangely, for female eccentrics but not male eccentrics there was a significant direct relationship between self-reference and creativity. Creative eccentric women tended to be more self-referencing, whereas those whose eccentricity did not take a creative form were less self-referencing.

Eccentrics are not only more self-referencing than normal people but also much more so than any of the clinical groups of mentally ill people studied by the psychiatrists who formulated the TLC scale. They included well-diagnosed patients suffering from mania, schizo-affective disorder, and schizophrenia. Indeed, the only group that may be as highly self-referencing as eccentrics is children, who tend to use even more first-person pronouns than schizophrenics do. Is it possible that the eccentrics' high levels of egocentricity and self-concern in their speech are simply manifestations of their innocent, even childlike vision of themselves and their worlds?

While it is usually impossible to do any sort of psycholinguistic investigation of people from the past, for the obvious reason that we rarely have audiotapes of them speaking (and when we do, it is generally formal public speech, which does not lend itself well to this sort of analysis), it is perhaps worthwhile to have a look at their more intimate, impromptu writings in the light of the insights of psycholinguistics. William Blake was a voluminous letter writer, and the following extract from a letter to his dealer, Thomas Butts, dated November 22, 1802, has the spontaneous feel of the spoken word. The letter is remarkable not only for the eccentricity of its religious subject matter but also for the way it is expressed. It is heavily self-referencing and has the driven single-mindedness of eccentric speech. It might even be said that it is an example, though written rather than spoken, of pressured speech, so obsessively do the words tumble forth:

> . . . Tho' I have been very unhappy, I am so no longer. I am again Emerged into the light of Day; I still & shall to Eternity Embrace Christianity and Adore him who is the Express image of God; but I have travel'd thro' Perils & Darkness not unlike a Champion. I have Conquer'd, and shall still Go on Conquering. Nothing can withstand the fury of my Course among the Stars of God & in the Abysses of the Accuser. My Enthusiasm is still what it was, only Enlarged and confirm'd.

After a final paragraph devoted to business matters, Blake signed the letter and then added this postscript: "A Piece of Sea Weed Serves for a Barometer; it gets wet & dry as the weather gets so."

One may conclude from the psycholinguistic analysis of eccentrics that their communication disorders might better be understood simply as communication differences. That is not merely a semantic fig leaf: while eccentrics may be more prone to express their thoughts in strange and aberrant ways, they are not less eloquent for that. Much the same could be said about the great majority of all interesting verbal expressions. If there were such a thing as speech that was purely logical and completely devoid of any communication disorders, it would suffer from the worst linguistic defect of all: dullness. And while eccentrics may at times be infuriating, absurd, and puzzling, they are never, never dull.

TEN

Eccentric Women

Women's Affections are eccentrick to common Apprehension: whereof the two poles are Passion and Inconstansy.
—Baker's Chronicles

My moods were not permitted. First they were called premenstrual histrionics. Then they were called premenopausal histrionics.
—Veronica, a modern eccentric

NEARLY ALL PSYCHOLOGICAL PHENOMENA MANIFEST SOME DEGREE OF sexual dimorphism, and eccentricity is no exception. Our study pointed up several key differences in the course that eccentricity takes in men and women. While the rate of incidence is about the same, the ways in which eccentricity expresses itself in the sexes are very different, revealing profound psychological differences between them.

The first striking disparity emerged from the historical

analysis, in which male eccentrics accounted for more than 85 percent of the sample. There were a number of obvious factors to be taken into account, all relating to the changing role of women in society. During most of the period covered by the historical sample, 1550 to 1950, women were only rarely public personalities and were thus far less likely to be written about in the public records we drew on. Their place was very much in the home, and few of them had the option of choosing any life for themselves other than the submissive and subsidiary role assigned them by society.

Moreover, fully a quarter of the historical women eccentrics were noted for their outstanding beauty and wealth. The former point may reflect the male bias of the sources; we rarely found out if the male eccentrics were good-looking or not. The latter is a reminder of the power and independence—and impunity from criticism—bestowed by wealth, all conditions that conduce to the emergence of eccentricity.

Until the seventeenth century, women who were different were often called witches, and tortured and killed. In more recent times they were likely to be labeled mad and shut away in institutions. When men were the sole guardians of the family's name and fortune, it was almost unthinkable to confine the head of the household in an asylum, for the result was often shame and destitution for the family. Many of the men in the historical sample were kept at home, where they were allowed to indulge their eccentricities harmlessly, in order to avoid such a disastrous social stigma. Even a recognizably crazy aristocrat or wealthy landowner might be given more charitable labels, such as "indisposed"—or "eccentric." Embarrassing wives, mothers, and daughters, on the other hand, were more expendable. They could more easily be gotten rid of by packing them off to institutions; in wealthy homes, governesses were responsible for child-rearing, and servants performed many of the household chores, making it not a terribly difficult matter to get rid of inconvenient female relatives.

Sex-related inequality in society's tolerance of aberrant behavior persists. Statistics from studies of alcoholic dependence show that only one out of ten nondrinking wives of alcoholics leaves her husband, whereas if the wife is an alcoholic nine out of ten husbands leave. Psychiatry, too, continues to regard aberrant behavior in women as more needful of treatment than the same activities in men. Fighting, leaving home for a couple of days, or going on a drinking spree, for example, may all be overlooked if the subject is a man, but a woman indulging in such behavior is likely to face questioning, harassment, and even institutionalized "treatment" against her will.

A recent study of hospital admissions found that men outnumbered women in state-run institutions, while admissions of women to private mental hospitals were disproportionately higher. One possible explanation for these figures is that the state hospitals have tight, standardized criteria for admissions, whereas the private hospitals are able to accept people whose illnesses are milder and might not even require hospitalization. The prevalence of female admissions to private institutions might suggest that women are referred more often for treatment of minor indications of mental illness that would be overlooked in a man—a genteel, contemporary version of the institutional dumping of inconvenient ladies.

The upshot is that we probably lost a large segment of our historical female eccentric population to locked gates and padded cells, and the psychiatric double standard that put them there is still with us.

It is now a truism that society puts greater pressure to conform on women than it does on men. Conventional parents raise a daughter to be a perfect wife and mother, while there is little similar emphasis on bringing up boys to become good husbands and fathers. Boys have traditionally been encouraged to display originality, aggressiveness, and initiative, whereas girls have been expected to be docile and helpful. While these patterns are shifting in many parts of society, it is nonetheless true that it takes a good deal more courage for a woman, particularly a woman born into a traditional home, to express her eccentric tendencies.

That courage to stand alone against society is well exemplified by Yvonne X, inventor of killer perpetual-motion machines. Before the machine blew up, she told me, "Why can't a woman be an inventor? If we can make babies, we can make gizmos. I know my theories seem far-out to some folks, but the right to be flaky is guaranteed by the Constitution. In 1990 the president proclaimed this to be the Decade of the Brain. Who do you think he was talking about?"

But times, and society's reactions, have indeed changed. Take the case of white witch Dot Griffiths, for example. Once she would have been adjudged a pagan heretic and given a trial by ordeal, drowned if "innocent" or burned at the stake if "guilty" or stubbornly unrepentant. But here she is today, based in bland Milton Keynes, England, next door to the Open University, able not only to practice her Wicca magic with her husband Reg, but also to act as a revered mentor, to teach her acolytes any number of arcane spells and potions, and to pass them on to anyone willing to learn.

We found in the study that a man is more apt to be eccentric beginning in his youth, while a woman may not reveal her strangeness until later in life. While she is married, and as long as her children are young, the woman conforms to standard social mores so as not to disrupt the life of the household. But when the children leave home, she feels free to let loose her eccentric, creative side, and often divorces her husband so that she can devote herself full-time to her hobbyhorses. This process of calculated fulfillment of the person's needs, wishes, and fantasies is usually called "flowering" or "blossoming." Male eccentrics, on the other hand, are more likely to be bachelors, and to have more numerous, briefer romantic relationships. They also have more marriages and more separations and divorces. The men themselves acknowledge that they make difficult partners for all but the most tolerant and understanding of women to live with.

The eccentric women in our study tended to be more curious, radical, experimenting, and aloof than the men. We found few female eccentrics who could be classified as scientists; most of them were of the wealthy recluse type, for the obvious reason that they could afford to indulge their whimsies. Many of the reclusive women in the historical sample would today be likely to be diagnosed as agoraphobic, while the reclusive women in our study tended to withdraw out of choice rather than fear. A few of them pointed out that there seemed to be a double standard, that it was more socially acceptable for a man to lead a solitary existence than for a woman to do so, especially a woman of what once was known as "marriageable age." Anita, an artist, told us:

> People think that just because I'm a woman, I must be caring, nurturing, and "people-oriented." They just can't believe that I prefer my own company. They don't realize that my happiest times are when I'm alone with my painting and music. They think I'm compensating for not being coupled by throwing myself into my work. My friends and family say they worry about me because I don't go out. I don't think male artists are quizzed so much about their social lives. People respect their need for solitude. When a male artist says he wants to shut himself off and create, they say he's serious about his work. When I do it, I'm either being selfish or I have a psychological problem.
>
> I really shocked one woman when I told her I didn't want to have children. She got angry, and said that she had two lovely daughters and wouldn't trade them for the world. She stewed for a long time, and then she said she had me figured out—my creations were my "children." Can you believe that? How would she like it if I told her that she had children to make up for the fact that she can't draw?

We discovered the greatest extent of sexual dimorphism in the degree of aggressiveness. The men were more aggressive than normal, but the women came up with extraordinarily high numbers: nearly 40 percent were found to be at the maximum level of this trait (see Table 8.1, page 181).

It may be that it takes a woman with a very aggressive personality to hold her ground in the face of social pressure and buck the female stereotypes. It is also possible that the sexual dimorphism is actually built into the system, and that the woman's behavior might be labeled as extremely aggressive simply on account of her sex. It is another modern truism that when men and women behave aggressively, especially in business, the man will be praised as dynamic and enterprising, while the woman will be criticized as abrasive and pushy.

Alternatively, it may be that some women gained a reputation for being eccentric simply because they were aggressive. Some of the older women in the study became social outcasts for making choices early in life that now seem acceptable and even ordinary, but that at the time were a mark of aggressive, unfeminine willfulness, shocking to family and friends:

An exclusive women's club invited me to join. Refusal was unheard of. I refused.

I divorced a man my family liked, and then married one they hated. I think they were especially infuriated because I didn't give a fig about their opinion. I always told my children I didn't care what they chose to do with their lives so long as it was legal.

After being condemned for actions that were nonconforming but altogether correct in their own eyes, these women made a conscious decision to become more eccentric. The world repeatedly told them that they were strange for behaving sensibly, so, exhilarated by their newfound sense of freedom and independence, they decided that they liked being strange. Being ostracized, rather than seeming like a punishment, made them feel liberated, which in turn inspired them to become even odder. Their behavior bespoke an attitude of "You want odd? I'll show you odd!"

Thus women who might initially have been considered eccentric simply for rejecting traditional female roles are gradually pushed into full-blown eccentricity. If Lillie Hitchcock Coit were alive today, she would undoubtedly be a firefighter. But as a little girl growing up in San Francisco during the Gold Rush, her obsession with fire engines and the life of the fireman was considered to be a bizarre rebellion. By the time she was ten, she was chasing after fire engines. In her late teens she was made an honorary member of the Knickerbocker Engine Company No. 5. For the rest of her life she put a "5" after her name, and she always wore the gilded badge of the company. After a fire, she would invite the firemen, still begrimed with soot, to a lavish meal at one of the city's finest restaurants. It was the era of Emperor Norton, Oofty Goofty, and the Great Unknown, and this most eccentric of American cities made Lillie Hitchcock its darling.

She married a wealthy businessman named Benjamin Howard Coit, but the marriage soon foundered on the jagged rocks of her eccentric behavior. One day she bleached her hair a garish shade of yellow with peroxide. When her husband objected, she shaved her head and wore red, black, and blond wigs, according to her whim, an even more shocking assertion of her individuality. Mr. Coit took her on a round-the-world cruise, hoping to cure her of her waywardness, but when they returned she went right back to Knickerbocker No. 5.

Next it was her father's turn to try to curb her flamboyance. Embarrassed by her antics, he set her up at a country estate in Napa Valley, miles away from the city. She responded by transforming it into a retreat for artists and writers passing through California; Robert Louis Stevenson was frequently her guest there while he was writing *The Silverado Squatters*. (Stevenson's wife, Fanny Osbourne, was similar in many ways to Lillie. Ten years older than Stevenson, she was a cigarette-rolling, pistol-packing American girl with a face, according to Stevenson, like "a Napoleon with insane black eyes.")

Mr. Coit disapproved of this bohemian coterie and left in a huff. On her own at last, Lillie returned to San Francisco and resumed her position as the city's mascot. Like so many eccentrics, she lived to a lusty old age; when she died in 1929, at the age of eighty-seven, she left her fortune to the city, whose citizens built a tower on top of Telegraph Hill in her honor. Though the architect stoutly denied it, to many San Franciscans Coit Tower resembles nothing so much as a Brobdingnagian fire-hose nozzle.

Because of the far greater social pressure for women to conform to a subservient role, particularly in previous eras, eccentricity in women has been inextricably intertwined with feminism. The feminist connection is stronger the farther back in time one looks. We have already mentioned

ECCENTRICS

Victoria Claflin Woodhull and her sister Tennessee; several more nineteenth-century feminists might be cited along with them, for their bold effort to overturn the established order is closely akin to the courage and vision that are required to become openly eccentric. There is a great behavioral chasm between women who were born before World War II and those who have been brought up in an era of increased tolerance of female independence and individuality. Among the younger women in our study, eccentricity developed in ways that were closer to those of men than was the case with the middle-aged and elderly women, who were raised in more conservative, old-fashioned homes.

Ironically, the social compulsion for women to conform reached its all-time high in a period named for a woman, the Victorian era. It is still widely believed that eccentricity reached its pinnacle then. Certainly Victorian eccentrics did things on a scale never seen before, with single-minded insouciance and flamboyance. Equal and opposite repression was as extreme, if not pathological, in its denial of sexuality and the female form. The fairest part of the world was ruled by a woman who was able to say, "The Queen is most anxious to enlist everyone to join in checking this mad, wicked folly of Woman's Rights, with all its attendant horrors." However, Queen Victoria miscalculated: nothing is so irresistible to eccentrics as an apparently hopeless quest, and to women like the Claflin sisters the words "mad, wicked folly" were an intoxicating elixir, not a deterrent.

Another such a one was Mary Kingsley (1862–1900), one of the most intrepid nineteenth-century explorers in Africa.

221

Like all Victorian girls, she had a sheltered childhood. Her father, George Kingsley, was an erratic anthropologist who traveled widely; Charles Kingsley, her uncle, was one of the most influential and widely read authors in Britain. She may have inherited her pluck and daring from her eldest uncle, Gerald, a sea captain who died at sea surrounded by the corpses of his crew, following a ghastly eighteen-month ordeal aboard his stinking, fever-ridden ship.

Like many eccentric children, Mary loved to play at scientific experiments; once, while attempting to make gunpowder, she blew up a tub of manure over a laundry line full of clean clothes. She was almost uneducated, except for a knowledge of German, which her father taught her so that she could assist him with his research. Most eccentric for a well-bred young lady of her class, she dropped her H's. She was exceptionally shy as a young woman, and spent morning till night doing housework, for her mother had taken to her bed as an invalid.

After her father died, Mary blossomed overnight into a full-blown eccentric. At the age of thirty, she decided to go to Africa to complete some of the research her father had left unfinished. At first she had no particular aim; her academic friends advised her simply to focus on "fetish and fish." She displayed classic eccentric curiosity. On her first voyage she acquired the nickname "Only Me" because of her habit of turning up in the engine room, the bridge, and almost everywhere else passengers were prohibited, in order to learn how things worked, always announcing her arrival with the words "It's only me."

Kingsley fell in love with Africa, and embarked on a series of travels more densely packed with thrilling adventures than anything a pulp novelist would dare to write; that she is not as well known today as Speke, Livingston, or Burton can only be attributed to an enduring antifeminine bias. She journeyed through western and equatorial Africa, discovering numerous species of fish that are named after her. She wanted to see native Africans who were completely unspoiled by contact with "civilized" whites, and that meant visiting cannibals. She was the first European to enter the part of Gabon then inhabited by the Fang, a tribe feared throughout West Africa for their ferocity. Yet polite, tenacious Mary Kingsley gained their confidence and secured an escort of Fang warriors to lead her through their territory.

For the Fang, cannibalism was no mere ritual but a food strategy. In one village she was accorded the honor of staying in a chief's hut, where she was surrounded by bags filled with drying human ears, toes, hands, "and other things." Nonetheless, by the end of her journey through the land of the Fang, she considered them to be "an uncommonly fine sort of human being."

Kingsley was a true feminist, in that she made it her aim to do everything that a man could do, only better. Other explorers, including Sir Richard Burton, had climbed the 13,760-foot peak of Mount Cameroon, but they had all taken the easier, western, side of the mountain. She chose the more difficult, southeast, face. She recorded in her journal, "I am the third English man [sic] to have ascended the Peak and the first to have ascended it from the south-east."

Rudyard Kipling, who knew her, said, "Being human, she

must have been afraid of something, but no one ever found out what it was." Her exploits were so incredible that when she published her memoirs, *Travels in West Africa,* in 1897, she left out some of the most hair-raising bits lest the whole book be dismissed as a pure fabrication. However, when she gave her immensely popular public lectures, she restored these ripping yarns, such as the one about the rampaging gorilla that charged her, her Fang guide shooting him point-blank in the chest when he was only yards away. And then there was the time a crocodile tried to crawl into her canoe, and actually got its front feet into it before she gave it a clout over the head with her paddle. Feminist or not, Mary Kingsley was a loyal daughter of the British Empire, and she died of fever while nursing soldiers in the Boer War.

A treatise published in 1682, called *The Ten Pleasures of Marriage,* warned against permitting women to "lordize" over their husbands, "because that, both by Heaven and Nature is given unto him," and under no circumstances was a wife to be allowed to wear trousers, even when her lord and master was not at home. Eccentrics will flout any convention that offers itself, and wearing trousers has been a perennial favorite. George Sand was among the earliest and remains perhaps the most famous woman to go out in public places dressed as a man. Many of her best novels have a strong feminist subtext, which has only recently been exposed by French literati and other critics, with the twenty-twenty vision of hindsight.

In America, Mary Walker, a nurse in the American Civil

War, campaigned against the "vile corset," which constricted women in more ways than one, and habitually went about in male formal attire. She was arrested several times for cross-dressing, but Congress awarded her the Medal of Honor for heroism and passed a special law allowing her to wear trousers. Walker was equally upset by "evil nicotine," and she would bat cigarettes from the mouths of surprised smokers on the street with her furled umbrella.

One of the most bizarre cases of cross-dressing must be that of James Barry (c. 1795–1865), a woman who lived almost her entire life passing as a man. It was an age when women were not permitted to study medicine, so, encouraged and abetted by her radical parents and their friends, in her early teens she adopted the name James (we do not know her real name) and matriculated at Edinburgh University, sixty years before women officially could be enrolled. She was considered something of an infant phenomenon at Edinburgh, and audaciously prefixed to her thesis (about *hernia cruralis*) this quotation from the Greek poet Menander: "Do not consider my youth, but consider whether I show a man's wisdom."

In 1812 she qualified as a doctor and took a commission as a surgeon in the British army, where she served for the remainder of her very full and vigorous life. While serving in Cape Town, Barry cut a very strange figure. She wore a heavily padded scarlet uniform, and was always attended by a manservant called "Black Sambo" and a little dog called Psyche. She became a close friend of the colonial governor, Lord Charles Somerset, a forty-nine-year-old widower. After she saved his life by correctly diagnosing typhus, the two seem to have had a love affair, and one recent biographer has even made the case that Barry left for a long voyage to the more liberal island of Mauritius in order to have his baby. Five years later, irony of ironies, the two were accused in the House of Commons of having committed sodomy, though the case seems never to have been brought to trial.

There were several close calls throughout her career. A midwife working with James in Cape Town reported that when she rushed into "his" bedroom to seek his help during a medical emergency, she got a peek and testified, "Dr. Barry was and is a woman." When Barry was very ill with yellow fever in Trinidad, she instructed her own doctors not to examine her under any circumstances, and if she died she was to be buried immediately, still dressed in her clothes. A young surgeon, concerned by her condition, disobeyed these peculiar orders. He found her out, and cried "See! Barry is a woman." She awoke and immediately summoned the presence of mind to swear him to secrecy. She was eventually promoted to the post of inspector-general of public health, from which eminence she campaigned for better and more humane conditions for all her patients, particularly women, the poor, and the native people under her care. That enterprising aggressiveness, and persistent suspicions about "Dr. Barry's peculiarities," eventually led to her dismissal, without any of the usual honors.

The question of James Barry's sex remained unsettled even after her death. Mrs. Sally Bishop, the woman who was called in to lay out the body, publicly declared that the deceased was a woman, but the doctor who attended Barry in her final illness said that as far as he was concerned, James Barry was a man. Another expert medical examiner, a Professor Kirby, wrote,

> Although Dr. Barry was essentially male in character, he undoubtedly possessed external characters that were sufficiently feminine in appearance to deceive the average person who happened to see him either partially or fully clothed. . . . I therefore consider that Dr. James Barry was definitely male, though one who was unfortunately feminine in external appearance.

It's hard to believe that such a confused and confusing statement was acceptable, or even intelligible, to those who read it. Professor Kirby seems to be making a suggestion of hermaphroditism, a very rare combination of sexual attributes, but more likely he believed it was impossible that a person who successfully lived life as a man could not be one. We shall never know for certain, but there is no reason to doubt Mrs. Bishop, who exclaimed with disgust that "it was a pretty doctor, not to recognize a woman's corpse when he saw it."

ELEVEN

Sexual Eccentricity

Love consists in this
that two Solitudes protect and
touch and greet each other.

—*Rainer Maria Rilke*

WHERE DYSFUNCTION IS ABSENT, MANY PEOPLE ARE RELUCTANT TO
discuss sex, one of the most intimate aspects of life, with a
stranger such as a psychologist. Therefore it was difficult for
us to glimpse much of the sex lives of the eccentrics in the
study beyond the basic facts that would be known to a
census taker.

Eccentrics are usually friendly people, glad to share their
hobbyhorses with anyone who is interested, but they tend
to be solitary by nature and sometimes find it difficult to be
intimate with other people. Nonetheless, most of them do
cherish romance when and if it comes along, and fall head

over heels in love, but when the initial enthusiasm wanes, they have a hard time sustaining the relationship.

We also found that a rather large number of modern eccentrics seem to have no particular interest in sex. Loners such as Anita, the artist, have chosen celibacy and seem to be genuinely contented with that way of life.

Beyond the high rates of divorce and celibacy, we had no indication that the sexual practices of eccentrics deviated much from those of the rest of the world. That finding may be the result of society's increasing permissiveness toward sexuality, for any definition of eccentricity depends upon the prevailing standard of acceptable behavior. In classical Greece, for example, it was not only acceptable but a common practice for grown men to seduce young boys, with the consent of their parents, and to have them as lovers. The Greeks believed that such a relationship, which may have arisen from prehistoric initiation rites, was beneficial to the boy. Today we consider pederasty completely unacceptable, based on the opposite assumption, that it is harmful to the boy, and those who practice it are regarded not as eccentrics but as criminals (though people such as Lewis Carroll, who felt strong pederastic impulses but sublimated them into socially acceptable channels, likely were eccentric).

The prevalent, though by no means universal, view of sexual behavior today may be briefly summarized: anything goes, so long as no one is hurt and all parties are competent to consent. By this standard, many sexual activities that were once classified as symptoms of mental illness, personality disorder, or perversion, are now considered to be harmless by most (though, again, not all) people. These changes took place after research in the postwar period, led by Alfred Kinsey and others, discovered that there was considerably greater variation in human sexual behavior than was known or publicly admitted to. Yet even before Kinsey, the expression of sexuality had been becoming more and more liberal since before the beginning of this century.

Nonetheless, homosexuality was considered taboo throughout the English-speaking world until quite recently and classified as a mental illness until the 1970s, although it has always been widely practiced. It was only one instance among many of psychiatrists functioning as "thought police" and agents of social control. More bizarre forms of sexual behavior such as sadomasochism and fetishism are now thought by some psychologists to be, under certain conditions, harmless and acceptable sexual expressions. Where anything goes, eccentricity becomes a meaningless concept. Today, therefore, any activity outrageous enough to fall outside the normal range is more likely to be regarded as a symptom of sexual dysfunction than as eccentricity.

Yet in the first decades of this century, when homosexuality was still widely proscribed, it was probably almost as prevalent a practice as it is today. The widespread experimentation with homosexuality at British public schools, while harmless in most cases to boys who were heterosexual by nature, left their gay schoolmates in a predicament: the experience brought out their homosexual inclination, which was illegal, and left them with no socially acceptable outlet for it. Homosexuals in the first part of the twentieth century had two choices: concealment, which made them prey to blackmail and other forms of victimization and, if they married, to tremendous feelings of guilt; or open expression, which carried with it grave risks.

The latter, of course, was the choice of eccentrics. In England between the wars there emerged an irregular subculture of gilded young aesthetes, many of whom were openly gay when that was a decidedly eccentric thing to be. Stephen Tennant, a beautiful young artist of modest talents, the beloved of the poet Siegfried Sassoon, was literally gilded: he sprinkled gold dust in his hair. Ronald Firbank wrote a series of precious, whimsical novels with titles such as *The Artificial Princess, The Flower Beneath the Foot,* and *Concerning the Eccentricities of Cardinal Pirelli* (the eccentricities referred to in the latter included serving coffee in chamber pots). He wrote his novels in hotel rooms, surrounded by clouds of hothouse flowers, using a quill pen on stacks of blue postcards. According to Osbert Sitwell, at a lavish dinner in Firbank's honor the novelist refused to eat anything except a single green pea.

While Tennant and Firbank were undoubtedly eccentrics, many of the other gay young things in their circle may have simply been members of a subculture, adhering to an alternative canon of social conventions. Their "flamboyant lifestyle," as it would be called nowadays, was a reaction against a grimly normalizing society that did not accept them as they were.

That sort of prejudice, of course, was largely the product of the Victorian era in Britain and the United States. A hun-

231

dred years before there was a far greater tolerance of aberrant behavior, if it was politely and discreetly expressed. If Lady Eleanor Butler and her friend and companion, Sarah Ponsonby, had been born a hundred years later, they might have suffered the same fate as Oscar Wilde. The two ladies met probably in 1774, fell passionately in love, and made a covenant between them to withdraw from the world and devote themselves entirely to each other. Lady Eleanor was the daughter of an Irish peer, and Sarah Ponsonby, a Dublin gentlewoman ten years her junior, was just twenty-one years old when they met. They ran away together at once, but their relatives found them, brought them home, and tried to dissuade them. However, they were determined, and in 1778 they went to Wales to search for a place of retirement. They settled upon a cottage in the Welsh village of Plasnewydd, in the vale of Llangollen, where they lived in complete seclusion with their maidservant, Flirt the dog, and Mrs. Tatters the cat; neither of them spent a single night away from the cottage until their deaths fifty years later.

The Ladies of the Vale, as they were known to their rustic neighbors, lived self-sufficiently upon a tiny income, raising much of their food themselves. Always dressed in men's clothes, Lady Eleanor and Sarah passed their days doing chores, tending the garden and the chicken coop, baking, making wine, and carrying out a wide array of self-improvement projects. Sarah Ponsonby described this idyllic existence in a letter to a friend:

In the Mornings after breakfast I try to improve myself in drawing. . . . My B. [Beloved] is also improving herself though that is scarce possible in Italian—She also Amuses herself with Compiling and transcribing Notes illustrative of her admired Madame de Sevigné. After dinner She reads aloud to me 'till nine o'clock when we regularly retire to our dressing room . . . where we generally employ ourselves 'till twelve.

The romantic friendship of the Ladies of the Vale and their utopian way of life endeared them to intellectuals throughout Europe. Their visitors included Wordsworth, Southey, De Quincey, Scott, Josiah Wedgwood, and the Darwins; the Duke of Wellington was a close friend. They became so famous that Queen Charlotte herself asked for the plans of their cottage and garden.

Exactly what the ladies' dressing-room employments consisted of no one knows, nor would it have occurred to anyone at the time to ask. It was, after all, a century before Queen Victoria famously refused to sign a bill that outlawed female homosexuality, declaring that such a thing could not exist. The biographer of the Ladies of Llangollen, Elizabeth Mavor, never uses the words "homosexual" or "lesbian," choosing rather "to portray the relationship between the two women in other terms than Freud's."

Their passionate love for each other constituted a large part of their appeal to their contemporaries. Certainly their journals were filled with the most ardent effusions, even when compared with the flowery expressions of friendship that were common at the time. Eleanor's epithets for Sarah seem to come from the *Kama Sutra:* "The Beloved of My Soul," "The Delight of My Heart," "The Joy of My Life."

Their bound journals had the initials E.B. on the front and
S.P. on the back, as did their china and nearly everything
else they owned. Eleanor, who was prone to migraines,
filled her journal with entries such as this one:

> I kept to my bed all day with one of My dreadful Headaches.
> My Sally, My Tender, My Sweet Love lay beside me holding
> and supporting My Head till one o'clock. . . . Mrs. Tatters
> uneasy that we did not come down Stairs at the usual hour
> Scratched at our Door for admittance, came on the bed to
> me and lay there till Ten o'clock at night Purring all the
> Time—a day of Tenderness and Sensibility.

Elizabeth Mavor gently suggests that such postmigraine tenderness and sensibility may have been code for sexual
activity. While society greatly approved of romantic friendship between women, it was nonetheless strictly circum-
scribed. The tenderest demonstrations of affection were
permissible and even sanctioned, but if it had ever become
known that the ladies' friendship was sexual (if indeed it
was), then social opprobrium would have come crashing
down on them.

The Ladies of the Vale conducted their friendship in private, and it could hardly have been a more discreet and
innocuous affair; yet some flagrant sexual abnormalities
were also tolerated in the eighteenth century, or at least
permitted to be practiced so long as the participants were
upper-class males. At midcentury, a dissolute lord named
Sir Francis Dashwood (1708–81) founded the Hell Fire Club
at Medmenham Abbey, a ruined monastery on the banks of

the Thames in Buckinghamshire. There he and his acolytes in debauchery met for blasphemous rituals that almost certainly included sexual orgies. According to one eyewitness, "The cellars were stored with the choicest wines, the larders with the delicacies of every climate, and the cells were fitted up for all the purposes of lasciviousness, for which proper objects were provided."

Dashwood surrounded himself with an inner circle of twelve, in order to parody Jesus and the apostles, and they called themselves the Monks of Medmenham. There was also a lower order of attendants to swell the rout and wait on the blasphemers when they celebrated their black masses. While the contemporary chroniclers all assure us that the Hell Fire Club's proceedings were depraved in the extreme, they forbear to tell us exactly what went on. Morbid George Selwyn was one of their number; another member was John Wilkes, who later became a popular advocate of libertarianism in Parliament. (The *Dictionary of National Biography* states that Wilkes's older sister, Sarah, "was an eccentric recluse—prototype of the Miss Havisham of Charles Dickens's *Great Expectations*.") Legend has it that Wilkes was responsible for breaking up the Hell Fire Club, when he smuggled in a baboon, which was "dressed in the fantastic garb in which the childish imagination clothes the Devil." At an appropriate point in the black mass, Wilkes unleashed the ape upon the celebrants, and scared them out of their wits.

In periods when there was great social pressure to limit sexual practices to a narrow range, those who wished to engage in taboo activities simply did so in secret. Yet eccentrics cannot resist an opportunity to flout convention openly, or at least to bend the rules to the breaking point. For instance, we have already examined female transvestism, which in the case of James Barry may not have been essentially sexual in nature. While it is true that she practiced transvestism with the intent to deceive rather than to outrage, it was a very open deception, which carried with it great risks—risks that ultimately overtook her. In the beginning she was driven by an overwhelming desire to practice medicine, yet as she became accustomed to life as a man she may well have found it personally and even sexually satisfying; perhaps if she had lived in the late twentieth century she would have changed her sex surgically. George Sand and Mary Walker, on the other hand, wore trousers flauntingly, as a political statement. If it did play a part in their sex lives, it is unlikely that we shall ever know.

Cross-dressing is one aberrant activity that society finds more acceptable for women than for men. Thanks to dress reformers such as Sand and Walker, most people now react with scarcely a raised eyebrow to the sight of a woman in a man's dinner jacket; Marlene Dietrich made it not only acceptable but chic. Men who like to dress as women, on the other hand, are subject to severe opprobrium. We are amused by comic actors in drag—Milton Berle and Barry Humphries, to name two famous examples, or Cinderella's Wicked Sisters in a Christmas pantomime—exactly because we know it is only make-believe. The audience experiences a sensation of exhilaration at seeing the taboo being openly broken, yet the antic nature of the representation prevents it from becoming a threat. Likewise, the heterosexual man who comes to a Halloween party wearing a woman's dress is likely to be the brawniest, hairiest man at the party, to reinforce the irony and make it clear that it's only in fun. If the other partygoers thought that the temporary transvestite was getting a sexual thrill from his costume, then they would cease to enjoy it.

Setting aside such facetious examples, transvestism in men is most often a sexual expression—though it is now widely recognized that many, if not most, male transvestites are heterosexual. In the case of the Abbé de Choisy (1644–1724), cross-dressing was used as an ingenious method of seducing girls. Choisy's mother had already had three sons and longed for a daughter, so when her fourth child turned out to be a boy, she decided to bring him up as a girl, just as was the case with some of the modern eccentrics. Little François, the future abbé, was frequently dressed in girls' clothes, and his ears were pierced so he could wear earrings.

The king's brother Philippe, the duc d'Orléans, who was called Monsieur, was a frequent visitor *chez* Choisy. A notorious homosexual who frequently dressed as a woman in public, Monsieur was devoted to little François, who was always impeccably gowned and coiffured for him. Choisy later wrote a description of Monsieur that serves as an apt portrayal of many male transvestites: "It is impossible to describe the extent of his coquetry in admiring himself, putting on patches [*mouches*] and then changing their positions. . . . Men, once they think they are beautiful, are far more besotted with their appearance than women are."

Young Choisy found a great liking for female dress and

continued the practice into adult life. After his mother's death, when he was twenty-two years old, he devoted himself wholeheartedly to his passion. In his memoirs, written at the end of his life, Choisy devotes almost as much space to his couture and coiffure as to what he did while wearing them; even at the distance of fifty years, he was still able to remember the number and placement of his *mouches* on a particular evening.

Despite his effeminate upbringing, Choisy was lustily heterosexual. Nonetheless he was a disgrace to the family; after he began to appear in public dressed as a woman, his male relatives ordered him to put an end to it. Then his elder brother died and he inherited the family fortune, enabling him to move away from Paris and practice transvestism unreproached. He bought a house in the town of Bourges, where he successfully deceived all the local gentry into believing that he was the Comtesse des Barres, a recently widowed noblewoman. The mothers in the vicinity were only too eager to send their young daughters to visit Madame la comtesse, where they might learn about the latest Parisian fashions and hairdressing styles.

Once he had the girls under his roof, he was able to seduce them easily. Occasionally his ardent nature almost betrayed him. He describes one occasion when he was receiving guests while he was in bed, a common practice of aristocrats at the time, with his current favorite under the covers with him. He tells us that he surreptitiously made love to her while he chatted with his neighbors, until the girl moaned with pleasure and cried, at an inappropriate moment in the conversation, "Ah! that's wonderful!"

ECCENTRICS

In Paris, Choisy fell in love with a beautiful girl, whom he persuaded to dress as a man. With the full knowledge of the girl's family, they had a mock marriage: "Wearing a robe of silver moiré and a small bunch of orange blossoms behind my head, like a bride, I said in a clear voice, before all the relations, that I took Monsieur de Maulny for my husband." After a festive supper, the couple retired and "gave ourselves to joy, but without overstepping the limits of propriety. That may be difficult to believe, but it is nonetheless true."

The Abbé de Choisy's life in drag came to an abrupt end in 1683, when he fell gravely ill. In a feverish delirium, he made an oath to God that if he recovered he would mend his ways and lead a devout life. He kept his word, and for his last forty years he devoted himself to an unexceptionable life of religious service. His account of his travels as a missionary in Indochina, the *Journal ou suite du voyage de Siam,* is a classic of French travel literature. He also published an eleven-volume history of the Church and many other religious and historical works, but he reserved his greatest zeal for his *Transvestite Memoirs.*

Moving forward nearly three hundred years, the essentials of transvestism remain the same. Ed Wood, Jr. (1924–78), best known as the writer and director of *Plan 9 from Outer Space,* which is widely regarded by film cultists as the worst movie ever made, was a fanatical advocate of transvestism. Like the Abbé de Choisy, he was dressed as a girl by his mother when he was young. During World War II he served in the Marine Corps in the Pacific, where he was a heavily decorated hero, winning the Bronze Star, the Silver

Star, the Purple Heart—all the while wearing female undergarments beneath his uniform. He participated in the invasion of Tarawa, where four thousand Marines went in but only four hundred came back. Wood was one of the survivors. Afterward, he told one of his Marine buddies, "I wanted to be killed, Joe, I didn't want to be wounded, because I could never explain my pink panties and pink bra."

Wood's first feature film was an unabashed work of propaganda for transvestism called *Glen or Glenda.* It has also been shown under the titles *I Changed My Sex, I Led Two Lives,* and *He or She?* The film is a pseudodocumentary about the social oppression of transvestites, centered around the anguished story of a man obviously based upon Wood himself, interwoven with irrelevant scenes of Bela Lugosi as a demonic spirit, intoning portentous mumbo-jumbo.

Wood never had the slightest success as a filmmaker, for the simple reason that his films were bad. Recognition came after his death, when the worst of his movies, *Glen or Glenda* and *Plan 9 from Outer Space,* became camp classics. Yet throughout his life Wood displayed the classic eccentric trait of unsinkable optimism and tenacity in the face of continual disappointment. He was happily married to the same woman until his death, of a heart attack, at the age of fifty-four. He eked out his livelihood by writing trashy pornographic novels based upon the themes of his films, perhaps as many as seventy-five of them. He was not a good writer, either, but he had a goofy, uninhibited imagination that gave his novels a certain louche charm.

Drag Trade (1967) is typical. It tells the story of Raymond Gomez, who was dressed in pink dresses as a child and grows up to be "Sheila Gomez," a liquor-store stick-up artist in drag. Other characters include Martin Harmony, known professionally as "Mary Harmony, the Jell-O Girl," a female impersonator whose career selling stolen cars is interrupted by the FBI; Big Nellie, who runs a drag bar for whites only until a group of black transvestites holds a "swish-in" and forces him to integrate; and Yahio Mura, a Japanese "sister boy," or drag prostitute, who assassinates a politician with a samurai sword. From *Drag Trade* (the ellipses are Wood's):

> Life had been one long procession of dresses . . . seldom he wore the same panties more than once or twice . . . once the dainty garments entered water they lost their newness and feel . . . this is of the utmost importance to the transvestite . . . clothes are his very essence.

Sadomasochism veers closer to the line dividing eccentricity and neurosis. Its mildest form, light spanking in an otherwise affectionate relationship, may be nothing more than a harmless erotic stimulant. In its heavier forms, such as outright flagellation, it often stems from or manifests deep, neurotic feelings of unworthiness. T. E. Lawrence, the legendary hero of the Arabian theater of World War I, had a lifelong passion for being flogged. In *Seven Pillars of Wisdom*, his classic account of the guerrilla campaign in Arabia he helped lead during the war, Lawrence describes a brutal beating he received while the prisoner of a Turkish bey in

Der'a, Syria, after he repulsed the man's attempts to seduce him. After being severely whipped and sexually abused for an extended period, he received a vicious kick from the corporal supervising the torture: "I remembered smiling idly at him," wrote Lawrence, "for a delicious warmth, probably sexual, was swelling through me."

Throughout the rest of his adult life, Lawrence continued to seek gratification of his masochistic impulses. After his death, the full extent of his aberrant behavior was revealed when a fellow from his outfit, a Scotsman named John Bruce, wrote to T. E.'s brother Arnold Lawrence. Bruce said he wanted to get in touch with Lawrence's uncle. Arnold was nonplussed, as he and his brother had no living uncles. Bruce explained that T. E. had approached him and asked for his help in a family matter. Lawrence told him that he had committed a crime against his uncle or his uncle's wife, the exact nature of which was never revealed, and the uncle had agreed not to press charges if Lawrence subjected himself to a private regimen of corporal punishment.

John Bruce, a brawny, naive country lad, agreed to give Lawrence a series of floggings, for which Lawrence paid him. Lawrence told him that after each of the beatings, he went to a doctor who examined his welts and wrote the uncle to certify that the punishments were sufficiently severe. These floggings continued over a period of twelve years. Lawrence's modern biographers have made the logical assumption that the beating he received in Der'a had not only humiliated him, leaving him with an ineradicable feeling of pollution, but had also implanted in him the idea that

242

pain and pleasure were inextricably connected. The notion of single-trial, traumatic associative learning is a fairly common explanation for the symptoms of masochistic pathology.

Whether or not T. E. Lawrence's sexual kinks ought more properly to be considered as the product of neurosis, his personality was certainly that of an eccentric. In 1918 King George V summoned the returning war hero for a private audience, to decorate him with the Order of the Bath and the Distinguished Service Order. Lawrence politely refused them, leaving the shocked king, in his own words, "holding the box in my hand."

Another dedicated masochist was the Australian-born piano virtuoso and composer Percy Grainger (1882–1961), whose works include "Country Gardens," a beloved musical staple for generations of school concerts and pageants. Grainger exhibited a whole cluster of sexual eccentricities. He was dominated by a powerful mother whose devotion to him constantly verged on the incestuous, and may have actually crossed over the line. He had deep homosexual tendencies, with an obsession for very young girls thrown in for good measure. Yet Grainger's greatest passion, like T. E. Lawrence's, was flagellation, though he preferred to whip himself. When he was on recital tours, he brought dozens of whips with him and always laundered his shirts himself, because they frequently had bloodstains on them.

What was most remarkable about Grainger's obsession with the whip was his extreme candor on the subject. He insisted that there was nothing sick about his activities, however unusual they were. His doctor wrote,

Whip-lash marks were not infrequently evident at the time of his examinations and treatments at the office. The explanations were readily forthcoming, and as the years went by I gradually learned his own conception of himself. He would never ask me to try to cure him. He did not consider it a disease. He considered it something that might be deplored by some, yes, but it was also something to be enjoyed by him. He could not help it. To him it represented a biological characteristic given to him to be exercised with no social infringements and with enormous personal joy. In addition he had the gift of music; these two precious talents he felt should be exercised to the fullest.

Grainger's love of flagellation stemmed from his exaggerated views of what constituted manliness. In 1936 he wrote to a friend, "A man cannot be a full artist unless he is manly, & a man cannot be manly unless his sex-life is selfish, brutal, willful, unbridled." This extraordinary view expressed itself in many ways: when he was living in Germany, Grainger would regularly open all the windows of his study in the dead of winter and lie spread-eagled on top of his piano completely naked. He also held racist views about the superiority of the white race, which in some ways anticipated Nazism; he rinsed his hair with peroxide all his life in order to maintain a perfectly blond, Nordic appearance.

Grainger undoubtedly stretched the definition of eccentricity far into territory ordinarily reserved for sexual neurosis. But it is possible that he did not stretch it beyond the breaking point: he never subjected others to his strange passions, and it is certain that he enjoyed them mightily. Still, his obsessions were bizarre. He once wrote to a German girlfriend to explain the sort of relationship he envisioned with his children, if he should ever have them:

> I propose this: Never to whip them till they are old enough to grasp the meanings of lots of things, then to say to them: Look here! I want to ask a favour from you kids. I want to whip you, because it gives me extraordinary pleasure. I don't know why it does, but it does. It gladdens me more than eating even. I know it's rotten for you, but then: I am particularly kind to you kids. I've worked hard to make you free in life, so that your childhood not only may be jollier now than ordinary children's, but may last ever so long. . . . I say to you: I'm kind & a good old thing, & polite & obliging. Now why not do me a great favour, as one equal to another, let me whip you; because, only, it gives me such unexplainable delight. Don't you think the children'd let me? I have hopes. . . . You know that I long to flog children. It must be wonderful to hurt this soft unspoiled skin . . . & when my girls begin to awaken sexually I would gradually like to have carnal knowledge with them. . . . I have always dreamed about having children & whipping them, & to have a sensual life with my daughters.

As horrifying as this document will be to most people, it should be emphasized that it was pure fantasy: Grainger

never had any children, nor came close to it. What is particularly eccentric about it is not the outrageousness of what
he proposes but rather that he had the nerve or the naiveté
to express it explicitly to a woman who, presumably, might
have been the mother of the children he wished to whip
and have sex with.

TWELVE

Eccentricity and Health

The last thing we find out when writing a book is what we must put first.

—*Blaise Pascal,* Pensées

THE ECCENTRIC PROJECT WAS THE MOST CHEERFUL RESEARCH ANY psychologist ever undertook. With few exceptions, the subjects in the study were happy, even joyful people, and their joy was infectious. Yet not even psychology, softest of sciences, could attempt to prove such a subjective but strongly felt assertion as the one we have made on several occasions in this book—that eccentrics are happier than the rest of us.

Nonetheless, there are some objective standards we can apply to evaluate this claim. In the first place, the simple pleasure of being able to do as one pleases without worrying overmuch about social repercussions is self-evident even to the strictest logician. Also, eccentrics draw strength and joy from their sense of humor. They themselves stressed to us time and again that humor and laughter were essential for their sense of well-being and their self-esteem in an increasingly dreary, conformist world. It also proved to be the means by which they could make light of their personal failings. This playful attitude toward life became more and more valuable to them as their lives progressed.

Moreover, eccentrics have more to be happy *about:* the single quality most often associated with happiness in the popular mind is good health, and there is ample evidence that eccentrics are healthier and live longer than the rest of us. The eccentrics in the historical sample, which covered the period from 1551 to 1950, lived to sixty and beyond during times when people were fortunate to live to be thirty-five. Modern eccentrics rarely visit a doctor, and when they do it is almost always for the diagnosis and treatment of moderately serious health problems. The eccentrics in our sample averaged one consultation every eight years, far fewer than the general population. In Great Britain, for example, where there is a free national health service, the average person goes to the doctor twice a year—sixteen times more often than the eccentric does.

One obvious explanation that presents itself is not as circular as it appears at first: eccentrics are healthier because they are happier. There is a more satisfying way of expressing this idea, which is based upon neurochemistry. Stated simply, eccentrics experience much lower levels of stress because they do not feel the need to conform, and lower stress levels mean that their immune-response systems can function more efficiently. Of course, there are all kinds of stress, including some that are beneficial. Positive forms of stress, such as those associated with sex, exercise, and the intellectual excitement of new ideas, have been found to trigger the release of slightly more growth hormone, which helps keep us young.

Eccentrics may well have slightly higher levels of growth hormone, which would mean that they are less susceptible to the diseases associated with old age, such as osteoporosis (weakening of the bones) and muscle atrophy. Growth hormone has also been shown to have a good effect on memory, and eccentrics even tend to look younger than their biological age.

But other forms of stress have a deleterious effect on the nervous system. When the mind perceives that the organism will fail to adapt in a given circumstance, the body activates its neuroendocrine-stress system. In other words, it is not the stimulus itself that induces stress but rather the individual's interpretation of it, especially the conviction that he will not be able to cope successfully. An American football player, fearless on the gridiron, may wilt under the pressure of filming a ten-second television spot, whereas the rest of us would be swamped by stress-associated hormones if we were expected to return a kickoff against the San Francisco 49ers.

When the body senses that a massive failure to adapt is about to take place, the pituitary gland releases adrenocorticotrophin, which stimulates the adrenal cortex to produce cortisol, the most important stress hormone. Cortisol helps the body to prepare itself for an emergency, which is a good thing if you are actually faced with one. However, where a perpetual fear of failure in nonessential contexts creates a state of hormonal emergency, the result is chronic stress: anxiety, depression, and an overworked immune system.

The evidence is growing that the immune system is closely linked with the nervous and endocrine systems: these are the three major integrative biochemical networks in the body. For instance, nerve cells have certain endocrine properties, including the ability to secrete hormones. The three systems are a partially closed feedback loop engaged in continual "cross talk," which maintains a state of equilibrium. That equilibrium becomes upset under stress, which makes the body more susceptible to illness and causes it to respond more slowly to injury. People suffering from chronic stress take longer to recover and get back to normal.

Eccentrics, however, are largely immune to the physiological toll of stress, because they do not feel the need to conform, and typically are not concerned about how the rest of the world views them. Placed on the football field in the example above, an eccentric would simply run away with the ball, in whichever direction struck his fancy, and not particularly care whether people laughed at him. Because eccentrics simply avoid situations in which they may fail to perform successfully, or do not acknowledge failure when it occurs, their endocrine systems function without the destructive overproduction of cortisol and other stress-related hormones, leaving their neuroendocrine and immune systems in a state of delightfully unimpaired equilibrium.

The creativity of eccentrics feeds their insatiable curiosity with new and ever more fascinating questions. It is very involving, and helps to assuage, in part, their intellectual needs. It helps them to use their solitude constructively, whenever it occurs; in this respect, as a group they have few peers. These factors are vital contributions to their personal mental health, and both can be rewardingly emulated by us less daring noneccentrics.

Loneliness is fast becoming one of the great psychological scourges of our time. Having no outlet for the creative urge can be as stifling and ultimately as depressing as the effects of poverty: it is a deeper deprivation, of the mind and the spirit. Similarly, the habits of mind induced by popular mass culture have promoted so much boredom, such deep feelings of powerlessness, that we would do well if we could exchange our excessive material acquisitiveness for the eccentrics' inner inquisitiveness.

Their forthright enthusiasms and wildly diverse interests give them the energy to feel young without being narcissistic. Their feverish activity works for them. They play what is in essence a game of brainstorming for one. By expressing their creativity for a long time and in many ways, they have overcome any feelings of rejection, unfairness, and anger they may have harbored earlier. Their spontaneous solutions to their problems dissipate the bases of neuroses in a way that gives fulfillment to them, and amuses those lucky enough to witness their *joie de vivre*. If you could distill what the essence of human happiness is all about, this would be it.

Societies, too, exist in a state of equilibrium, though they are open systems, not closed loops. Without innovation and fresh ideas, they atrophy and lose their competitive edge. Eccentrics are essential for the health of the social organism, for they provide the variety of ideas and behavior that permits the group to adapt successfully to changing conditions. The theory of evolution might provide a useful analogy: Darwin never tired of saying that natural selection could accomplish nothing without heritable variation. In the opening pages of *On the Origin of Species,* he wrote, "A high degree of variability is obviously favourable, as freely giving the materials for natural selection."

Eccentrics are the mutations of social evolution, providing the intellectual materials for natural selection. And what is more readily heritable than a new idea? If there is one trait of the eccentric that plays an essential role in social health, it is originality. It is self-evident that all intellectual evolution depends upon new ideas; they are the essence of science, of exciting new art, indeed of all intellectual progress. This book has recounted many instances of eccentrics who have discovered strikingly new ways of thinking. Of course, some of their ideas seem to us absurd or misguided, yet they may not be more so than some of the byways of "straight" science and philosophy.

It is a paradox: on the one hand, a society cannot function—indeed, it cannot actually be a society—without some degree of agreement, and a lot of unremarkable conformity. Yet on the other hand, a successful society must have wide enough scope for nonconformity to keep from withering intellectually and slowly stifling under a blanket of oppressive uniformity. In the medieval church calendar, no festival was celebrated more avidly than the Feast of Fools, when the rites of the church were blasphemously parodied, and public drunkenness and every kind of lewdness were permitted to go on. In every part of the world, from the earliest times, royal courts had jesters, usually teched and deformed entertainers who were allowed to say any outrageous nonsense that popped into their heads—even, or especially, to the monarch himself. These officially sanctioned eccentrics served as a sort of safety valve, satisfying the perceived need for a nonconformist presence in the culture. Thus, even in the most autocratic, rigidly conventional civilizations, there was an awareness that absolute uniformity was harmful to the social organism.

In the English-speaking nations, there has been, at least fitfully, a greater tolerance for nonconformist thinking. England has become proverbial throughout the world as the haven for eccentrics, and as we have found, the United States gives it very strong competition. The exceptions to this generalization are well-known: Cromwell's England and Puritan Massachusetts were as oppressive as any societies that ever existed. But they are notable precisely because they are exceptions, and in both cases there were present the seeds of rebellion and reaction.

The notion that a man's home is his castle, and that what goes on there is his business and no one else's, is fundamental to English (and thus American) law. Freedom of speech and the opportunity to behave oddly with impunity are conducive to eccentricity, and may even provide the minimum background conditions for it to develop. In countries where extremes of behavior are not appreciated, or are persecuted, it takes more strength and force of character to push back the boundaries and to deviate from the norm.

All men and women, even those whose lives appear on the surface to be thoroughly conventional, invent themselves to a very great extent. Man is unique in the ways that he does not come to terms with his environment. Every other species adapts by passively responding to its environment, the place where it happens to have been born. In contrast, man is what he chooses to be. Eccentrics take that basic human prerogative of free choice and force it to the limit. They ceaselessly assert and reassert their fundamental right to be what they want to be.

Eccentrics are people who take a boundless joy in life, immoderate men and women who refuse to violate their ideals. Their minds are always buzzing furiously with ideas. They may fail in a particular endeavor, but society wins by their example, and by what can be salvaged from the exotic ideas and seemingly unanswerable questions that they propagate with such enormous energy. At the root of eccentricity is a healthy and determined irreverence. It is utterly harmless, and a source of decency, tolerance, and respect for different views and different people.

This research has shown that certain types of deviant behavior can be healthy and life-enhancing. The condition of eccentrics is freedom: not for them the stifling habit of obedience. In an era when human beings seem more and more to be the prisoners of their culture and their genes, eccentrics are a refreshing reminder of every person's intrinsic uniqueness. By flouting norms of behavior that most of us never question, eccentrics remind us how much of our own liberty we needlessly forfeit, and how great is our ability to forge our own identities and shape our own lives, if only we will use it.

BIBLIOGRAPHY

Aaronson, B., and H. Osmond, *Psychedelics* (London: 1971).

Acton, Harold, *Memoirs of an Aesthete* (London: 1984).

Adams, Patch, "Building a Chuckle: How to Be a Nutty Doctor," *Mothering* 38 (winter 1986), 29–32.

———, *Gesundheit!* (Rochester, Vt.: 1993).

———, "The Happy Paradigm, or Oh Gosh, Here it Comes," *Holistic Medicine*, March/April 1987, 16–18.

———, "How About a Paradigm for Happiness?," *Holistic Medicine*, November/December 1986, 15–16.

———, "The Practice of Medicine is Fun," *Holistic Medicine*, November/December 1987, 10–11.

———, "What Would Play Be Like if There Was Sustained Peace on Earth?," *Holistic Medicine*, July/August 1986, 12–15.

American Psychiatric Association, *Diagnostic and Statistical Manual of Mental Disorders*, 3rd ed. (Washington, D.C.: 1980).

Andreasen, N. C., "Scale for the Assessment of Thought, Language and Communication," *Schizophrenia Bulletin* 12/3 (1986), 473–81.

———, "Thought, Language and Communication Disorders: II, Diagnostic Significance," *Archives of General Psychiatry* 36 (1979), 1325–30.

BIBLIOGRAPHY

Andreasen, N. C., and W. M. Grove, "Thought, Language and Communication in Schizophrenia Diagnosis," *Schizophrenia Bulletin* 12/3 (1986), 348–59.

Archer, J., "The Influence of Testosterone on Human Aggression," *British Journal of Psychology* 82/1 (1991), 1–28.

Arnheim, R., *Visual Thinking* (Berkeley, Calif.: 1969).

Asimov, Isaac, "Editorial-Eccentricity," *Science Fiction* 12/4 (April 1988), 4–8.

Bakan, P., "The Right Brain of the Dreamer," *Psychology Today,* November 1976, 66–68.

Barnes, B., and D. MacKenzie, "On the Role of Interests in Scientific Change," in R. Wallis (ed.), *On the Margins of Science: The Social Construction of Rejected Knowledge. Sociological Review* monograph 27 (1979), 49–66.

Barron, F., *Creativity and Personal Freedom* (Princeton, N.J.: 1968).

Beer, Thomas, *The Mauve Decade* (New York: 1961).

Berlitz, Charles, *The Mystery of Atlantis* (New York: 1976).

Bhaskar, R., *A Realist Theory of Science* (Brighton, U.K.: 1978).

Bird, John, *Percy Grainger* (London: 1976).

Blake, William, *Complete Writings,* ed. Geoffrey Keynes (London, Oxford, and New York: 1969).

Boston, R., *The Admirable Urquhart* (London: 1975).

Boswell, James, *The Life of Samuel Johnson, LL.D.,* ed. Alexander Napier (London: 1884).

Bridgeman, Harriet, and Elizabeth Drury, *The British Eccentric* (London: 1975).

Carson, Robert C., James N. Butcher, and James C. Coleman, *Abnormal Psychology and Modern Life* (Glenview, Ill.: 1986).

Cattell, R. B., *Personality and Motivation: Structure and Measurement* (New York: 1957).

Cattell, R. B., H. W. Eber, and M. M. Tatsuoka, *Handbook for the Sixteen Personality Factor Questionnaire* (Champaign, Ill.: 1970).

Caulfield, Catherine, *The Emperor of the United States and Other Magnificent British Eccentrics* (London: 1983).

Chesler, P., *Women and Madness* (New York: 1972).

Choisy, Abbé de, *The Transvestite Memoirs,* trans. and with introduction by R.H.F. Scott (London: 1973).

Churchward, James, *The Children of Mu* (New York: 1968).

———, *The Sacred Symbols of Mu* (New York: 1968).

Clark, J. H., *A Map of Mental States* (London: 1983).

Clark, Kenneth, *The Nude* (London: 1956).

Crawford, H. J., "Hypnotizability, Daydreaming Styles, Imagery Vividness, and Absorption: A Multidimensional Study," *Journal of Personality and Social Psychology* 42/5 (1972), 915–26.

Current, R. N., *The Lincoln Nobody Knows* (New York: 1958).

De Camp, L. Sprague, *Lost Continents* (New York: 1954).

Demos, J., "Underlying Themes in the Witchcraft of Seventeenth-century New England," *American Historical Review* 75 (1970), 1311–26.

Desmond, Lawrence Gustave, and Phyllis Mauch Messenger, *A Dream of Maya* (Albuquerque, N.M.: 1988).

Dillon, K. M., B. Minchoff, and K. H. Baker, "Positive Emotional States and the Enhancement of the Immune System," *International Journal of Psychiatry in Medicine* 15/1 (1985–86), 13–18.

Donnelly, Ignatius T. T., *Atlantis: the Antediluvian World* (New York: 1882).

Dorson, R. M., *America in Legend* (New York: 1973).

Durndell, A. J., and N. E. Wetherick, "The Relation of Reported Imagery Tests to Cognitive Performance," *British Journal of Psychology* 67 (1976), 501–6.

Eiduson, B. T., *Scientists: Their Psychological World* (New York: 1962).

Erikson, K. T., *Wayward Puritans* (New York: 1966).

Feyerabend, Paul, *Against Method: Outline of an Anarchistic Theory of Knowledge* (London: 1976).

Firbank, Ronald, *Five Novels,* with introduction by Osbert Sitwell (New York: 1981).

Fothergill, Brian, *Beckford of Fonthill* (London: 1979).

———, *The Strawberry Hill Set* (London: 1983).

BIBLIOGRAPHY

Friedrich, Otto, *Glenn Gould* (New York: 1989).

Galton, F., *The Art of Travel* (London: 1855).

Ghiselin, B., *The Creative Process* (Berkeley, Calif.: 1952).

———, "Ultimate Criteria for Two Levels of Creativity," in C. W. Taylor and F. Barron (eds.), *Scientific Creativity: Its Recognition and Development* (New York: 1963), 141–55.

Goldstein, L., "A Reconsideration of Right Hemisphere Activity During Visual Imagery, REM Sleep, and Depression," *Research Committee in Psychology, Psychiatry, and Behavior* 9/1 (1984), 139–48.

Grey, Rudolph, *Nightmare of Ecstasy: The Life and Art of Edward D. Wood, Jr.* (Los Angeles: 1992).

Guinn, J. M., "Some Eccentric Characters of Early Los Angeles," *Historical Society of Southern California Publications* vol. 5 (1902), 273–81.

Hall, J. A., *Nonverbal Sex Differences* (Baltimore: 1984).

Hartmann, T., and O. Havik, "Exploring Curiosity: A Curiosity-Exhibitionism Inventory, and Some Empirical Results," *Scandinavian Journal of Psychology* 21/2 (1980), 143–49.

Hastings, Selina, *Nancy Mitford* (New York: 1985).

Henderson, B. B., S. R. Gold, and M. T. McCord, "Daydreaming and Curiosity in Gifted and Average Children and Adolescents," *Developmental Psychology* 18/4 (1982), 576–82.

Henderson, D., and R. D. Gillespie, *Textbook of Psychiatry* (Oxford: 1962).

Henry, T. R., *Wilderness Messiah* (New York: 1955).

Holmberg, A. R., *Nomads of the Long Bow* (New York: 1969).

Hooper, J., "Beeper Psychology," *OMNI* 8/8 (May 1986), 26.

Hosmer, J. K. (ed.), *John Winthrop's Journal, History of New England* (New York: 1908).

Houston, J. P., and S. A. Mednick, "Creativity and the Need for Novelty," *Journal of Abnormal and Social Psychology* 66 (1963), 137–41.

Hovanetz, "Auntie Barbara," *Auntie Barbara's Tips for an Ordinary Life* (New York: 1992).

Howard, E. M., and J. L. Howard, "Women in Institutions: Treatment in Prisons and Mental Hospitals," *Women in Therapy* (New York: 1974).

ISC Newsletter, various numbers (Tucson, Ariz., 1988–94).

James, Jamie, "Bigfoot or Bust," *Discover,* March 1988.

———, *The Music of the Spheres* (New York: 1993).

Jamison, Kay Redfield, *Touched with Fire* (New York: 1993).

Johnson, K., "The Court Jester of Modern Medicine," *East-West,* June 1987, 36–43.

Johnson O'Connor Research Foundation, *Personality Work Sample 35A Manual* (Chicago, 1977).

Jones, B., *Follies and Grottoes* (London: 1974).

Karson, S., and J. W. O'Dell, *Clinical Use of the 16PF* (Champaign: 1976).

Kegan, R., *The Evolving Self: Problems and Processes in Human Development* (Cambridge, Mass.: 1982).

Kendler, K. S., "Diagnostic Approaches to Schizotypal Personality Disorder: A Historical Perspective," *Schizophrenia Bulletin* 11/4 (1985), 538–53.

Kendler, K. S., A. M. Gruenberg, and M. T. Tsuang, "Psychiatric Illness in First-degree Relatives of Schizophrenic and Surgical-control Patients: A Family Study Using DSM-III Criteria," *Archives of General Psychiatry* 42/8 (1985), 770–79.

Khatena, J., "Autonomy of Imagery and Production of Original Verbal Images," *Perceptual and Motor Skills* 43 (1976), 245–46.

Klonsky, Milton, *William Blake: The Seer and His Visions* (New York: 1964).

Koestler, Arthur, *The Act of Creation* (New York: 1964).

Kramer, William, *Emperor Norton of San Francisco* (Santa Monica, Calif.: 1974).

Kubie, L. S., *Neurotic Distortion of the Creative Process* (Lawrence, Kans.: 1958).

Lane, Allen Stanley, *Emperor Norton* (San Francisco: 1939).

Leder, L. H., *America 1603–1789, Prelude to a Nation* (Minneapolis: 1972).

Lees-Milne, James, *William Beckford* (Tisbury, Wiltshire: 1976).

Lewin, B. D., "Remarks on Creativity, Imagery, and the Dream," *Journal of Nervous and Mental Diseases* 149 (1969), 115–21.

Longford, Elizabeth, *Eminent Victorian Women* (New York: 1981).

Loosen, P. T., S. E. Purdon, and S. N. Pavlov, "Effects on Behavior of Modulation of Gonadal Function in Men with Gonadotropin-releasing Hormone Antagonists," *American Journal of Psychiatry* 151/2 (1994), 271–73.

MacDiarmid, Hugh, *Scottish Eccentrics* (Manchester: 1993).

MacFarlane, A., *Witchcraft in Tudor and Stuart England* (London: 1970).

Mack, John E., *A Prince of Our Disorder* (Boston, Mass.: 1976).

Mackal, Roy, *A Living Dinosaur?* (Leiden: 1987).

Mackinnon, D. W., "The Nature and Nurture of Creative Talent," *American Psychologist* 17 (1962), 484–95.

Marais, E., "John the Painter," *New Society* 31 (1975), 643–64.

Marti-Carbonell, M. A., S. Darbra, A. Garau, and F. Balada, "Hormones and Aggression," *Archives de Neurobiologie* 55/4 (1992), 162–74.

Maw, W. H., and E. W. Maw, "Nature of Creativity in High- and Low-Curiosity Boys," *Developmental Psychology* 2/3 (1970), 325–29.

McGonagall, William, *Poetic Gems* (London: 1934).

McGuire, C., "Dimensions of Creativity," *Proceedings of the Southwest Psychological Association,* American Psychological Association (1958), 1–25.

Mednick, S., "The Associative Basis of the Creative Process," *Psychological Review* 69/3 (1962), 222–32.

Merton, R. K., *Social Theory and Social Structure* (New York: 1968).

Mitford, Jessica, *Daughters and Rebels* (New York: 1960).

Mitford, Nancy, *The Water Beetle* (New York: 1986).

Mitgang, H., *Lincoln as They Saw Him* (New York: 1956).

Moers, Ellen, *The Dandy* (New York: 1960).

Morris, P. E., and P. J. Hampson, *Imagery and Consciousness* (London: 1983).

Myerson, A., and R. D. Boyle, "The Incidence of Manic Depressive Psychosis in Certain Socially Important Families," *American Journal of Science* 98 (1941), 11–21.

Nash, G. B., *Red, White and Black* (Englewood Cliffs, N.J.: 1982).

Newell, A., J. C. Shaw, and H. A. Simon, "The Elements of a Theory of Human Problem Solving," *Psychological Review* 65 (1958), 151–66.

Nunn, C. Z., H. J. Crockett, and J. A. Williams, *Tolerance for Nonconformity* (San Francisco: 1978).

Olson, J., "Backward Is Forward," *Northern Student* vol. 11, September 24, 1986, 11–12.

Perkins, D., *The Mind's Best Work* (Cambridge, Mass.: 1981).

Plato, *Timaeus* and *Critias,* ed. Desmond Lee (London: 1971).

Poincaré, Henri, "Lecture at the Société de Psychologie, Paris," in B. Ghiselin (ed.), *The Creative Process* (Berkeley, Calif.: 1952), 39–40.

Popper, Karl, *Conjectures and Refutations* (London: 1963).

———, *The Logic of Scientific Discovery* (London: 1959).

Purser, P., *The Extraordinary Worlds of Edward James* (London: 1987).

Raine, Kathleen, *William Blake* (London: 1970).

Rambro, R., *Lady of Mystery* (San Jose, Calif.: 1967).

Rice, William B., *William Money: A Southern California Savant* (Los Angeles: 1943).

Roazen, Paul, *Brother Animal* (Harmondsworth, Middlesex: 1973).

Rolfe, Frederick (Baron Corvo), *Stories Toto Told Me,* with preface by Christopher Sykes (London: 1969).

Satie, Erik, "Memoirs of an Amnesiac," in *The Writings of Erik Satie,* ed. and trans. Nigel Wilkins (London: 1980), 57–66.

Scarr, S., and K. McCartney, "How People Make Their Own Environments: A Theory of Genotype-Environment Effects," *Child Development* 54 (1983), 424–35.

Scheff, T. J., *Being Mentally Ill: A Sociological Theory* (Chicago: 1974).

Schmaus, W., "Fraud and the Norms of Science," *Science, Technology and Human Values* 8/45 (1983), 12–21.

Seelig, Carol, *Albert Einstein* (London: 1956).

BIBLIOGRAPHY

Shackford, J. A., *David Crockett* (Chapel Hill, N.C.: 1956).

Sifakis, Carl, *American Eccentrics* (New York: 1984).

Simonton, D. K., *Genius, Creativity, and Leadership* (Cambridge, Mass.: 1984).

Sitwell, Edith, *English Eccentrics* (London: 1971).

Sperry, R. W., "Hemisphere Disconnection and Unity in Conscious Awareness," *American Psychologist* 23 (1968), 723–33.

Sternberg, R., *The Nature of Creativity* (New York: 1988).

Stone, L. J., and J. Church, *Childhood and Adolescence: A Psychology of the Growing Person* (New York: 1968).

Stone, M. H., *The Borderline Syndromes* (New York: 1980).

Swanson, G. E., and S. S. Phillips, "Schizotypic and Other Profiles in College Students: Some Social Correlates" (Department of Sociology and Institute of Human Development, University of California, Berkeley, 1984).

Taylor, Calvin W., and Frank Barron, *Scientific Creativity* (New York: 1963).

Thomas, K., *Religion and the Decline of Magic* (London: 1971).

Tyler, L., *Individuality* (San Francisco: 1978).

Tyrer, P., P. Casey, and J. Gall, "Relationships Between Neurosis and Personality Disorder," *British Journal of Psychiatry* 142 (1983), 404–8.

Uglow, J. (ed.), *MacMillan Dictionary of Women's Biography* (Bristol: 1982).

Uzick, L., "Anabolic-androgenic Steroids and Psychiatric-related Effects: a Review," *Canadian Journal of Psychiatry* 37/1 (1992), 23–28.

Vaughn, C. E., and J. P. Left, "The Influence of Family and Social Factors on the Course of Psychiatric Patients," *British Journal of Psychiatry* 129 (1976), 125–37.

Vernon, P. E., G. Adamson, and D. F. Vernon, *The Psychology and Education of Gifted Children* (London: 1977).

Virkunnen, M., et al., "Personality Profiles and State Aggressiveness in Finnish Alcoholics, Violent Offenders, Fire Setters, and Healthy Volunteers," *Archives of General Psychiatry* 51/1 (1994), 28–33.

BIBLIOGRAPHY

Wallas, Graham, *The Art of Thought* (New York: 1926).

Ward, J. W., *Andrew Jackson* (New York: 1955).

Waterton, C., *Wanderings in South America* (London: 1825).

Waxman, David, *Hypnosis: A Guide for Patients and Practitioners* (Winchester, Mass.: 1981).

Weeks, D. J., "Conceptual Structure in Hypochondriasis, Arthritis and Neurosis," *British Journal of Clinical Psychology* 24 (1985), 125–26.

———, "Eccentrics, the Scientific Investigation," *The Proceedings of the Royal College of Physicians of Edinburgh* (January 1989), 125–28.

———, "Thinking in Schizophrenia, Eccentricity, and 'Normality'—Whither Linguistics?" paper, annual conference of the British Psychological Society, Leeds, 1988.

Wing, J. K., J. E. Cooper, and N. Sartorius, *The Measurement and Classification of Psychiatric Symptoms* (London: 1974).

Ziman, J., *Public Knowledge: The Social Dimensions of Science* (London: 1968).

INDEX

INDEX

INDEX

INDEX

INDEX

INDEX

Minneapolis–St. Paul, 26
Mitford, Nancy, 172–75, 187
Mitford, Tom, 172, 173
Mitford girls, 172–75
Mohammed, 114, 119
Monboddo, Lord (Burnett,
    James), 102–4, 106–7
Money, William, 108–10
Monks of Medmenham, 235
moralizers/proselytizers,
    194–95
Mormonism, 114–16
Morton, A. S., 117–18
motivation
    of eccentric scientists, 105–6
    and historical sample, 59–61
Mu continent, 127–29
musicians, 82–85
"The Musician's Day" (Satie),
    83–84
mysticism, 114–19
    See also religion
myths, 114, 119, 122
    See also Atlantis myth
Mytton, Jack, 60–61

names, and differentness, 163
National Frumps of America,
    185–86
near-death experiences, 147–48
neurosis, 14, 149
new species, 96–97
Newton, Isaac, 92, 94, 113
Niedzwieki, Patricia, 205
Norton, Joshua Abraham, 3–6,
    7–8, 14, 40
nudism, 106–7

obsessiveness, 27, 180, 182–84,
    204–6, 210
occult, 130–31
Ohm, Georg, 107
oil spills, 105
On the Origin of Species
    (Darwin), 252

Oofty Goofty, the Wild Man of
    Borneo, 6, 7
optimism, 35–36, 240
*The Origin and Progress of
    Language* (Monboddo), 103
Osbourne, Fanny, 220
other self, 191–92
Ouida, 63
outrageous behaviors, 189–90

paranoia, 142
paranormal delusions, 146, 148
parents
    abusive/repressive, 166–67
    capriciousness of, 173
    and childhood of eccentrics,
        163–67, 171
    children of eccentric, 155–56
    and gender confusion of
        children, 163–64
    rebellions toward, 171
Parmenter, Ryan, 72
past lives, 116
pederasty, 229
peer relations
    and eccentric children, 168–69
    See also conformity
Peladan, Josephin (aka Sar), 82
perpetual motion, 33–35
perseveration, 201
personality
    and doing ordinary things in
        extraordinary ways, 178,
        192–95
    evaluations of, 27
    and extremes, 178, 179–80
    and rarity, 178–79
    and self-presentation, 177
    and special attributes, 178,
        180–87
    and unusual combination of
        attributes, 178, 187–92
Peru, ancient, 122
Peter, fantasies of, 149–52
photographic memory, 76

273